W9-BUT-309

STRATEGIES
FOR CORRECT WRITING

STRATEGIES
FOR CORRECT WRITING

PAUL FOURNIER

WITH CONTRIBUTIONS BY
HEATHER DAVIS

Strategies for Correct Writing

Pearson Education, 10 Bank Street, White Plains, NY 10606

The present work is an authorized adaptation of the Canadian
edition, entitled *Blueprints*, by Paul Fournier, Copyright © 2003
, Published in Canada by ÉDITIONS DU RENOUVEAU
PÉDAGOGIQUE INC.

Text credits: **Page 102:** "Surrogacy Case Ends in Court Battle
over Names on Birth Certificate," by Denise Lavoie with files
from Tom Arnold, *National Post* (Aug. 30, 2001), p. A10.
Reprinted with permission of *The Associated Press*. **Page 104:**
"Do Women Talk More," from "Women Talk Too Much" by
Janet Holmes in *Language Myths*, Laurie Bauer and Peter
Trudgill, eds. (Penguin, 1998), p. 45. Reproduced by
permission of Penguin Books Ltd. **Page 114:** "Persuasion: The
Process of Changing Attitudes," from *Psychology* (Canadian
edition) by R. A. Baron et al. (Toronto: Allyn & Bacon
Canada, 1995), pp. 672–673. Reprinted with permission of
Pearson Canada.
Illustration credits: Robert Dolbec
Book design and page layout: Le Groupe Flexidée Ltée

Library of Congress Cataloging-in-Publication Data

Fournier, Paul, 1955-
    Strategies for correct writing / Paul Fournier.
      p. cm.
      ISBN 0-13-178742-X
        1. English language—Rhetoric—Problems, exercises, etc.
2. English language—Textbooks for foreign speakers. 3. Report
writing—Problems, exercises, etc. I. Title.

PE 1408.F545 2004
808'.0428—dc22

                                                        2003060307

Printed in the United States of America
1 2 3 4 5 6 7 8 9 10–VHG–09 08 07 06 05 04 03

To Éloi,

For overcoming your disappointment when you found out there was not going to be a *Blue Prince* in this book.

To Emmanuelle and Romy,

For everything that is good in life.

CONTENTS

Organization   96

Part 3: Language Use and Expression   121

Clarity   122

Reader Friendliness   135

Appendix: Models

INTRODUCTION

TO THE TEACHER

Strategies for Correct Writing is a task-based tool that evolved from writing problems commonly found in developing academic or work-related writing and the writing of non-native speakers.

Strategies for Correct Writing breaks writing down into easy-to-identify components such as *insufficient data, topic sentences, relevance of content,* or *variety of sentence types.* Instructors can use any component to help students focus on the aspects of their writing that should be given priority.

This book presents the essentials of writing—Context, Coherence and Language Use and Expression—in a user-friendly feature: Blueprint boxes. Blueprint boxes are templates that allow students to visualize what is missing from their writing whenever they superimpose their own texts on a blueprint.

Strategies for Correct Writing is designed to be used both as an editing guide and as a writing guide:

- As an editing guide, the book allows the instructor to point to a problem by using a correction code in relation to the sections of the book. Each correction code comes with a checklist of questions in the inside cover of the book, along with page references.

- As a writing guide, *Strategies for Correct Writing* offers all the explanations needed to work on essays, business letters, job résumés and reports. Since the book stems from a real-life approach, any teacher who has ever tried to answer student questions such as *How can I make my text more coherent? How can I make this passage clear?* or even *What do you mean by an "idea" when you say you want a main idea?* will find the answers in *Strategies for Correct Writing.*

Real-life tasks provide practice for defining, comparing, examining cause and effect and explaining a process. Workshops provide many opportunities to discuss writing samples that range from appropriate models to eye-stopping errors drawn from students' writing such as *People who talk to their plants get better results unless they also need to be watered.* Problem-probe activities allow teachers to contrast acceptable models with poor ones and to point out what problems need to be worked on. Once the students are made aware of problems, they can focus on their individual learning needs. An Answer Key for the exercises, workshops, and problem-probe activities is available at http://www.longman.com/strategiesforwriting.

KEY FEATURES

Correction Codes

The correction codes presented on the inside front cover can be used on student copies to refer to common problems identified in the book. For example, a problem with Task (code = TASK) will come under the following header:

Questions that students should ask themselves are presented (also found beside each correction code):

Did you cover every element required by the task?
Did you define and stay within the limits of the topic?

Actions that students should take to check the most common sources of mistakes look like this:

> **COVER EVERY ELEMENT REQUIRED BY THE TASK**

These sections are illustrated with problems found in students' writing. Note that the Contents can be used as an expanded checklist.

Examples of problems are usually preceded by this icon: ⊗.

Examples where the usage is correct are preceded by this icon: ≫.

⊗ I think everybody has to look different.

≫ Plastic surgery has given rise to a whole generation of faces that cannot smile.

Blueprints

After writing their first draft, the students try to see if their own texts have followed the Blueprint or template. When the text does not match the Blueprint, the students will notice at a glance what they need to edit to ensure that their text can be built on a clear and coherent structure.

BLUEPRINT FOR TOPIC SENTENCE

Check if your topic sentence matches the Blueprint.

BLUEPRINT	YOUR FINISHED PRODUCT	
Use facts that do not relate strictly to your personal experience (the use of *I* or *I think* is rare). The idea can be developed or defined.	A **topic** that is easy to identify.	A **focus (controlling idea)** that will clarify the focus of your paragraph. Make sure there is a verb.

Problem Probe, Workshop, Practice

These sections allow students to analyze and correct problems in writing. *Problem Probe* focuses on common mistakes. The students should be encouraged to look at the Blueprint that is placed near the Problem Probe sections to see why the passage does not fit the Blueprint. *Workshop* presents problems or longer tasks that usually require group work. *Practice* involves exercises for student to complete.

Models

Models of appropriate writing, such as letters, essays and reports, are presented.

Usage Hints

Margin notes focus on a language point relevant to the topic.

TO THE STUDENT

A Walk Through This Writing and Editing Guide

Context, *Coherence* and *Language Use and Expression* are the three major components you should focus on when using this book. From these major divisions, writing is then broken down into elements that you can act upon. Each element can be referred to with the help of a correction code.

1. CONTEXT

In this part of the book, you will get help **paying attention to context:** understanding and meeting a reader's real-world expectations about your text. Understanding the background, checking the requirements of the task and ensuring proper format allow you to place your writing in its context.

Correction code:	**TASK AND FORMAT** To pay attention to the context for your writing, you will:	**After your first draft:**
(TASK) TASK	Make sure you cover every element required by the task.	Check if your text addresses the task and meets the format requirements (e.g., for a letter, essay, report or job résumé).
	Define and stay within the limits of your topic.	
(FORM) FORMAT	Use consistent format.	

2. COHERENCE

In this part of the book, you will see how to **connect content, structure and context.** You will get help in checking whether your text is coherent. **Coherence** means that a text has both relevant content and appropriate structure.

- **Relevant content** means that you choose ideas that are useful in covering the task and effective in leading to your conclusion. A reader will think you chose relevant content if the ideas you used in your text can be connected to the task you defined under Task and Format.

- **Appropriate structure** means that the reader can easily find your introductory elements, body paragraphs and a sense of closure. Each of these parts are in relation to the other parts of the text.

Correction code:	CONTENT To choose your ideas, you will:	After your first draft:
(REL) RELEVANCE	Keep only ideas that can be developed. Choose ideas related to task, purpose and topic.	Check if your ideas are useful in meeting task, purpose and topic.
(LOGIC) LOGIC	Keep your focus.	Check if your ideas offer consistent perspective (your ideas go together and are of the same level of importance).
(ACC) ACCURACY	Check accuracy.	Check if your ideas are accurate (the facts are true).
(EFF) EFFECTIVENESS	Choose effective ideas.	Check if your ideas are effective in leading to and showing why your conclusion is right.

Correction code:	STRUCTURE To structure your text, you will:	After your first draft:
(INT) INTRODUCTORY ELEMENTS	Include introductory elements by • giving background information or context. • stating task and purpose. • giving a general idea of text content.	Check if you gave some background, presented the task and purpose, and in longer texts, announced the main points.
(THS) THESIS STATEMENT	Work on your thesis statement (in essays).	Check (in essays) if there is a clear statement of the view you will defend.
(PAR) PARAGRAPH	Start a new paragraph. Check the paragraph unity.	Check if you need a new paragraph and if everything in the paragraph is about the same idea.
(TS) TOPIC SENTENCE	Identify the topic and the focus (controlling idea).	Check if there is a topic sentence that contains the topic and the focus of the paragraph.
(SUPP) SUPPORT	Offer credible support.	Check if there are enough relevant details to support your topic sentence.
(REF) REFERENCING	Quote properly.	Check if you quoted properly when using sources in your support.

Correction code:	STRUCTURE To structure your text, you will:	After your first draft:
(TRANS) TRANSITIONS	Use helpful transitions.	Check if you need transitions to guide the reader along the development of your ideas.
(CONC) CONCLUSION	End with a conclusion. Confirm your thinking. Point out what the reader should remember. Limit or expand.	Check if there is a conclusion that confirms your ideas, makes clear what the reader should remember and limits or expands the scope of your ideas.
(ORG) ORGANIZATION	Choose an organization pattern that is appropriate to task and purpose.	Check if the organization helps your reader (definition, comparison, process) and can be connected to task and purpose.

3. LANGUAGE USE AND EXPRESSION

In academic and work-related writing, your texts must be **clear and reader friendly**: The reader should not have to constantly make efforts to try to understand.

- **Clarity** means that your reader does not have to stop and ask, "What is this supposed to mean?"

- **Reader Friendliness** means that you keep your readers in mind and use a style that most readers will consider appropriate.

Correction code:	CLARITY To make sure that your text is clear, you should:	After your first draft:
(CL) CLARITY	Check the meaning of key terms.	Check if all terms and numbers related to your subject are correct.
	Choose terminology appropriate to the situation or context.	Check if the connotation or collocation is appropriate in the context.
	Select words that convey your exact meaning.	Check if you can improve your choice of words.
	Check unclear grammar. Check problems in sentence structure.	Check if the grammar or sentence structure might have another meaning that will confuse the reader.

Correction code:	READER FRIENDLINESS To make your text friendly:	After your first draft:
(RDF) READER FRIENDLINESS	Consider the audience.	Check if your text is not too technical for the potential readers.
	Use appropriate tone.	Check if your text remains polite.
	Be as short as possible (and as long as necessary).	Check if you can cut passages that do not have much meaning.
	Use varied sentence types.	Check if you have used varied sentence types (simple, compound, complex).

ACKNOWLEDGMENTS

Sincere thanks to Linda Power (Dawson College) for her special help; and to colleagues who offered feedback: Nathalie Comeau (Cégep de Rimouski), Sandra Cole (Cégep de Trois-Rivières), Kay Powell (Collège Ahuntsic), Robert Walsh (Cégep de Trois-Rivières). I would like to thank Sharnee Chait, Joyce Rappaport and Muriel Normand for their thorough contribution, as well as the efficient Flexidée production team. Thanks to Jean-Pierre Albert for his continuing support.

PART 1

CONTEXT

Task
Format

Whenever you write a paper in college or at work, you must pay attention to **context**. Context refers to the circumstances that make you write the text. A professor or a boss may have asked you to submit a report in three weeks or you may feel you have to respond to a colleague, business or customer.

Since readers have expectations that depend on context, your **task** is to cover what the readers need or want to know. The Task section helps you pay attention to the essential requirements in your writing.

In work-related and academic contexts, readers usually expect the development of a text to follow a relatively standard **format**. How can you ensure that you meet the requirements of proper formats?

Part 1 examines the basic expectations of readers under the Task and Format sections.

If the feedback from your instructor or classmates tells you to focus on TASK, use this section to check the following:

Did you cover every element required by the task?
Did you define and respect the limits of the topic?

COVER EVERY ELEMENT REQUIRED BY THE TASK

Be sure that your text covers every part of the task that was assigned. For example, in work-related reports, you may be asked to

- check the safety of ...

- discuss the budget for ...

- analyze the effectiveness of ...

- compare the efficiency of ...

- make a decision about ...

MORE HELP? See Relevance, p. 40.

In argumentative or in literary essays, you may be asked to

- recognize the main idea from a reading selection

- identify the writing techniques used by an author

- offer an analysis or critical interpretation of the selected reading

- use references that show you understood what you read.

In academic writing, some key words may be used in assigned questions. Some common key words are:

- *Discuss* – explore the most important characteristics or main points.

- *Illustrate* – give examples that clearly show your understanding of the material (for example, refer the reader to information mentioned in a reading selection).

- *Analyze* – divide the problem or case into parts or characteristics; explain the functions or characteristics of the main parts.

- *Argue* (in an argumentative essay) – express a point of view and support it.

- *Evaluate* – use criteria to be able to judge the good/strong or bad/weak points.

MORE HELP? See Definitions, p. 96, Comparison, p. 103, Process, p. 110.

LIMIT THE TOPIC

Make sure your text is not off-topic. Ask yourself these questions:

- What is the topic?
- Which of your ideas address this topic?
- Which of your ideas do not address this topic?

For example, if the topic is the participation of children in elite sports programs, can you see which of these ideas is hard to link with the topic?

1 Elite sports programs teach children and teenagers about life.

2 Athletes often buy fancy sports cars at an early age.

3 Young children's bodies are not ready for so many hours of training.

The second idea is off-topic because it does not discuss children in sports programs.

MORE HELP? See Relevance, p. 40.

BLUEPRINT FOR TASK

Answer the questions in the right-hand column.

BLUEPRINT	
• Did you meet the word limit? (500 words? 750 words?) • If you are writing a business letter, have you checked to see that there are no more than 10 lines per paragraph?	
• Did you respect other constraints such as using assigned criteria in your analysis? For example: 1. Have you quoted from sources if requested? 2. Have you looked at various studies? 3. Have you demonstrated your comprehension of assigned readings? 4. Have you attended a conference or a presentation?	
• What is the topic? 1. Which of your ideas address this topic? 2. Which of your ideas do not address this topic?	

MORE HELP? See Organization, p. 96, to review the structures that can help you include every part needed for a task.

If feedback from your instructor or classmates tells you to focus on FORMAT, use this section to check the following:

Did you check to see if you have used the correct format for the text (letter, job résumé, report, essay)?

USE CONSISTENT FORMAT

Be sure that your academic or work-related letters, job résumés, reports and essays have a consistent format.

LETTER FORMAT

Today it is common to send correspondence as files over the Internet. To keep your format from changing, you should set up your letters in **block style** by aligning all words at the left margin. Your letters will require fewer formatting changes when the person at the other end is using a different program or printer.

YOUR ADDRESS: Companies have letterheads. If you are writing a personal letter instead, put your address on top.

3203 SE Woodstock Blvd.
Portland, OR 97202

DATE: Place just below the address.

January 30, 2005

SUBJECT LINE: Optional, but useful in guiding the reader (perhaps a secretary who must decide whom the letter is going to; a person who wants to know if the subject is a priority). Say what the letter is about, but just write key words.

Ms. Ines Camacho
750 South Alder Street
Portland, OR 97205

INSIDE ADDRESS: Must be the same as the address on the envelope.

Subject: Science Fair

GREETING: Use *Dear Mr./Ms./Dr. + family name* if you know whom you are writing to. If not, avoid the outdated *To Whom It May Concern.* Instead, write *Attention: Director of Personnel* or *Dear Sir or Madam:*

Dear Ms. Camacho:

I am writing to invite you to our school's science fair. Over 150 students from Reed College will present science experiments and research that they have worked on over the school year. There will be booths on topics from genetically modified foods to cloning to hydrogen fuel for cars.

BODY: Write in block style. Do not indent the first word of a paragraph. Begin by summing up the situation and state the reason for your letter. Don't scare the reader away. Make your letter brief: keep paragraphs short (no more than ten lines long). Make the purpose of the letter clear.

The event will take place from 9 a.m. to 4 p.m. on Saturday, March 14, 2005, in the school gymnasium. The school is located at 3203 Southeast Woodstock Boulevard, and there will be free parking available for the event.

On behalf of all the participants, I sincerely hope that you are able to attend. I know the students really appreciate the support and encouragement of enthusiastic visitors. We look forward to seeing you there.

Sincerely yours,

Greg Harvard

Greg Harvard
Reed College Science Department

COMPLIMENTARY CLOSING: *Sincerely* and *Yours truly* are common phrases.

SIGNATURE: Sign your letter and type your name below your signature.

OTHER COMMON FEATURES: *Enc./Enclosure* indicates that you have put something else in the envelope; *cc* followed by a name or names tells the reader who else is getting a copy of the letter.

Enclosure: Program of the fair

GRAMMAR NOTE: Letters often end with *I look forward **to hearing** from you,* not *I look forward to hear from you.*

Always assume that your letter will first be read by a stranger who knows nothing about you or your topic. For instance, you should imagine that a secretary will have to figure out who should receive your letter.

CAN YOU STATE YOUR MESSAGE IN JUST ONE SENTENCE?

Before writing, you must be clear about what you want to say. Once your message is obvious to you, it will be easier to write your letter.

> I want to interview a professional who works in urban planning for my geography project.

WHAT DOES THE READER NEED TO KNOW ABOUT THE SITUATION?

When the reader opens your letter, he or she has no idea what it is about. Introduce the reader to the situation:

> I am a student at Lakeview College who is currently doing research for a geography project. The project involves a team of students who must create a proposal for a new park in Seattle. Our team decided that the best way to answer some of our questions is to interview an urban planner. Our teacher, Mr. Jackson, recommended you.

WHAT REASON DO YOU HAVE FOR WRITING?

There are many reasons for writing letters. In the opening part of your letter, you should write a **purpose statement**, a sentence in which you tell the reader why you are writing. Here are some reasons for writing letters:

- You need information (for example, from a university, or from a person who can help you with a college project).

  > I am writing to ask for information about the undergraduate program in Biology at your university.

- You are requesting something from the recipient (a refund, a meeting, repairs).

  > I am doing research for a school project and since I am very interested in your current study, I am hoping that you will be available to meet with me to discuss it further.

- You are sending a letter that accompanies a job application.

  > In response to your ad in yesterday's *New York Times,* I am sending you my résumé so that I might be considered for the position of Junior Sales Representative.

- You are informing people about something (for example, you are telling them about a business you just started, or are sending them information they asked for).

  > In response to your question about healthy eating, our research is only preliminary, but it seems to suggest that a good diet must include omega-3 fats.

MORE HELP? See the appendix for more models of letters.

A good letter tells the reader specific information right from the start. Discuss the three sample introductory paragraphs below with a partner to spot the two paragraphs that are too general to be of use.

1 I am writing this letter because I will explain my view on the projects I saw and tell you why one project is better than the other. To do this, I will compare them. First I will compare the difficulties I anticipate. After that, I will show you the advantages each project has to offer.

2 I am writing to ask for your assistance in funding our new library reading program. The program is called Reading for Life and aims to help children develop lifelong reading habits. This will be accomplished by hiring university students to read to children who come to the library once a week. Our program can only become a reality with the support of generous contributors.

3 Last week, you asked me to evaluate two proposals for funding. We can only fund one between the School Breakfast Program and the Rehabilitation Center. I have to choose which one is ready for funding and to recommend it for full funding. To make a good judgment, I have to compare the best qualities of each project and to find the best and worst aspects. I have to decide which project is more important to fund by paying attention to coherent facts and studies mentioned in the proposals.

DO YOU NEED TO PROVIDE MORE DETAILS?

After your introductory paragraphs, you need to give the reader more information or explanations. Follow your introduction with short paragraphs that will make up the body of your letter. Here are two examples:

1 Last year, thirty-two students were involved in the Reading for Life program. They spent on average an hour and a half a week with over 360 pupils from local schools. Our recruitment drive for this year is now under way.

2 For weeks now, we have been unable to get a full night's sleep. The sudden noises caused by planes that should not be authorized to land in Teterboro during the night have disturbed countless citizens. The airport authorities should deny all landing requests overnight and redirect them to Newark Airport to ensure that the citizens of Ridgefield Park are no longer sleep-deprived.

WHAT ACTION DO YOU EXPECT?

Very few people write letters without expecting something from the reader. In the last few lines of your letter, state what action you want the reader to take; or, if you are responding to a letter, verify that you have satisfactorily covered what the sender had requested. This will give a sense of closure to your letter.

1 Unless you pay within the next ten days, we will transfer your file to a collection agency that will add its own costs to your bill.

2 Rest assured that we will repair your product for free again should any new technical problems develop.

Check if your letter meets the requirements stated in the left-hand column.

BLUEPRINT	
1 Sender's address	
Date	
2 Inside address	
Subject line	
Greeting	
3 Body: • Did you check left margins for block style? • Does the reader know who sent the letter? • Does the reader know about the situation right from the start? • Does the reader know why you sent the letter? Have you written a *purpose statement*? • Does the reader know what to do about the letter? If necessary, specify when and how the reader should respond.	

1 Check **ABBREVIATIONS**. Don't abbreviate the name of the month. Check for consistency in other abbreviations (e.g., 1st, 2nd, 3rd/Ave., St.) and *CAPITAL LETTERS* (Days, Months, Street).

2 Check **PUNCTUATION**. No commas are needed at the end of a line in an address. The greeting is followed by a colon. Commas are informal.

3 Check **VERB TENSE**. Do you need the present progressive form of the verb? *I am writing …* To describe the situation, do you need the past tense? Is the present perfect tense needed?

• Is every paragraph short? Make sure that no paragraphs have more than ten lines. 4—• • Do you need to add more details or information? • Have you included some transitional words that can guide the reader? (See Transitions, p. 85) • Did you close by letting the reader know what action you expect?	

5—• Complimentary closing	
Signature	
Typed signature	
Enclosures (if any)	
cc (if any)	

4 Check **LEVELS OF LANGUAGE**. Some words that you would use with friends are not appropriate. See p. 136.

5 Check **SPELLING**. Adverbs are often created by adding -*ly* to adjectives. The adjective is *sincere*. Do not forget the *e* before *ly*: the correct spelling is *Sincerely*.

Workshop

Use the Blueprint to write a letter based on one of the following tasks:

- Write to a university to ask for information about a program.

- Write a letter to a manufacturer to complain about problems you are having with something you recently purchased.

- Respond to a customer who is interested in buying a service or product from the company or store where you work. Unfortunately, you have to tell them that the service or product they want is no longer offered.

- Write to a hotel to confirm your reservation.

- Write to a job applicant to tell her that you are unable to offer her a job at the moment.

- Write to a professional you wish to interview for a research project or for the college newspaper.

- Respond to a citizen who wants to sue the airport authorities because of aircraft noise.

Practice

Do you know which verb tenses to use in a letter? Choose the correct verb tenses.

1 Dear Sir or Madam:

I (write) _____ this letter because I will be visiting New York in

March and I (need) _____ information on art exhibits.

2 Dear Sir or Madam:

I (send) _____ you my résumé because I want to apply for

the bank teller position advertised in *The Sherbrooke Record* last Friday.

Although I (have) _____ no previous experience in banking,

I (enjoy) _____ customer service and have very strong math skills.

I (currently / work) _____ for Sports Plus

as a salesperson and cashier. My job includes (help) _____

customers find what they are looking for and ringing up their purchases at the

cash register.

E-MAIL FORMAT

Writing e-mail is similar to writing a letter except that e-mail is more conversational and less formal. You don't need to begin with a greeting or finish with your signature, although you can certainly include these. Studies show that people read more slowly from a screen than from a paper version, so make sure that your e-mail messages are short.

MORE HELP? See Reader Friendliness, p. 135.

Model E-Mail

Subject: Vietnam Progress Report

From: swallace@gengineers.videonet.com

To: bdouglas@oxfam.com

The report on progress in Vietnam is nearly finished. Most of the resettling and dam-building work is going as scheduled. I will send you the whole report by the end of tomorrow.

One last question: do you still want to refer to affected persons as AP's or as APP's the way you did in the last report?

SHORT SUBJECT LINES

Always include a subject line in your e-mail message. This way you can show with just a few words what your message is about. Subject lines are very useful in e-mail as they might help someone decide whether to open your message or to treat it as spam (unwanted mail) that they would delete without reading.

Compound adjectives and noun-modifying-noun structures can help you keep subject lines short. Here are some examples:

Rainy Day Plan
Teaching Application
Broken Air-Conditioner Complaint
Opening-Day Schedule
General Assembly Documents
Proposed Contract

MORE HELP? See Can a Noun-Modifying-Noun Construction Be Used?, p. 141.

JOB RÉSUMÉ

A résumé is a brief description of your education, employment history, or experience. An effective résumé can help you make it to the shortlist of candidates who get an interview. What can you do for an employer that another candidate cannot do? Approach your job résumé by answering that question because this is what the employer wants to know.

Model Résumé

PERSONAL DATA
Name
Address
City, State Postal Code (Zip Code)
Daytime telephone number
(or cell, pager)
E-mail address

POSITION APPLIED FOR/JOB OBJECTIVE (optional)
If you are responding to an ad or know that there is an opening for a position, state the title of the job. If not, you may want to state your employment objective.

EDUCATION
Place either work experience or education first, depending on which is most relevant for the job. (For college students, *Education* usually comes first.) List, starting with the most recent and continuing back in time, the schools you have gone to, including their locations, and the diplomas you obtained. Write *in progress* or *expected* if degree is not yet completed.

WORK EXPERIENCE
List the jobs you have had, starting with the most recent one. You may want to explain your job duties. (Do not write obvious aspects like *nurse: giving injections to patients, filling out charts.*) Mentioning summer jobs or part-time jobs can be useful until you start working in your field. These jobs show that you are reliable.

1— Bernard Wetley
638 Garcia Street
Santa Fe, NM 87501
505-555-6200
wetleyb@dot.com

2— Objective: To obtain a challenging position that requires proven skills in video technology.

3— EDUCATION
2007 (Expected)
Bachelor's Degree, Communication.
St. John's University, Santa Fe.

2003
University of New Mexico,
Santa Fe Summer program in Arts and Communication.

2001
High School Diploma
Lawrence High School, Taos.

4— EXPERIENCE
June 2004-September 2004
Assistant Production Coordinator
Freelance for the National Video Board of New Mexico. Oversaw and coordinated the work of camera operators, sound engineers, set designers, and video editors.

September 2003-June 2004
Part-time Clerk
Opus Supermarket, Taos.

July 2003-September 2003
Camera Operator and Video Editor
Freelance work for Star Media Corp., Taos.

... June 2002
Jury Coordinator
~~Freelance work for the Evergreen Video Festival (CO).~~ Wrote up
criteria and explained them to jury members. Transmitted results to
organizers and media.

May 2001-June 2001
5 Video Producer
Volunteer work for the Immigrants' Integration Center, Carlsbad, NM.
Wrote scripts, organized, shot, and edited a video for
Independence Day celebrations.

January 2000-May 2000
Lawrence High School
Web Site Designer
Performed volunteer work, helping non-computer literate teachers to
create their own web sites.

December 1999-January 2000
Ski Instructor
Owl's Head, Evergreen, CO
Gave weekend lessons to beginners, age 7-9. Ensured safety
procedures.

6 **SKILLS**
Fluent in English, French and Spanish.
Proficient in Word, Excel, PowerPoint.
Can work with different digitized editing technologies.
Hold an American Red Cross CPR (Cardio-Pulmonary Resuscitation)
Certificate.
Earned an American Red Cross Lifeguarding Certificate.

AWARD
2000
First Prize in the Hull Video Festival for the video *Monsoon Car Wash*.

7 **REFERENCES**
Available upon request.

MORE HELP? See the appendix for an additional model job résumé.

---

5 OTHER EXPERIENCE
If you have never held a paying job,
volunteer work can be mentioned.

6 ACHIEVEMENTS AND SPECIAL
ABILITIES
What are the things that may help
you get the job? For example, list
the languages you speak and the
computer software programs you
can use. Mention recent awards
you may have won (forget the
prizes you won in elementary
school and the snowmobile race
you won recently: they don't show
what you can do on the job).

7 REFERENCES
You may include the names of
people who can give you
references, but this is not usually
necessary as a first step. Do not
include names unless you have
contacted the people to obtain
their permission. They may have
recommended someone else for
the same job.
PORTFOLIO: For some jobs,
a portfolio showing your previous
work might be useful.

- Don't include your age, height, weight, a picture, or your SSN (Social Security Number).
- Don't lie.
- Don't write more than two pages. Most managers spend about a minute per résumé.
- Don't provide names of references. You would have to contact them each time you apply for a job.
- Don't use very specialized terminology unless you know for sure that someone who understands it will read your résumé. The people in the human resources department might not be familiar with the jargon.
- Don't format your document with margins or tabs if you send the text through e-mail.
- Don't use too many types of spacing and highlighting (font size, **bold**, *italics*).

Problem probe

What problems should you check as you edit your résumé? Look at the résumé that follows the list below. The list contains a sample of errors or omissions typically made by college students in their job résumés. Referring to the list, first circle the problems you can spot in the sample résumé. Then fill in the boxes with the numbers that correspond to the problems you have identified. Some numbers will be used more than once.

1 Add cell phone number, e-mail address and pager number if available.

2 Add more detailed information (for example, name of program, name of company or business, town, year).

3 Check abbreviations and capital letters.

4 Check for spelling and typing errors.

5 Describe duties and responsibilities, using meaningful action verbs that show what you can do. (See list, p. 19)

6 Don't include personal information such as your Social Security Number, age, height or health situation.

7 Don't go too far back in time. Use information that is still useful.

8 Use the correct English term.

9 Name the position you are applying for. If this is not possible, state your professional goals.

10 Place more recent information first when listing your education and experience.

11 Use a consistent system for spacing and highlighting. Your font, size, and use of bold and italics should follow an easy-to-identify pattern.

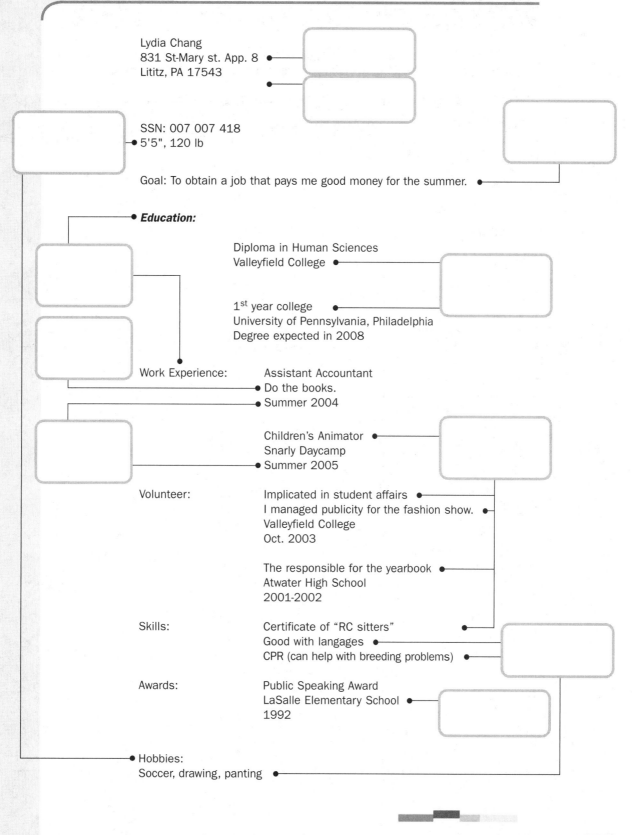

Lydia Chang
831 St-Mary st. App. 8
Lititz, PA 17543

SSN: 007 007 418
5'5", 120 lb

Goal: To obtain a job that pays me good money for the summer.

Education:

Diploma in Human Sciences
Valleyfield College

1st year college
University of Pennsylvania, Philadelphia
Degree expected in 2008

Work Experience: Assistant Accountant
Do the books.
Summer 2004

Children's Animator
Snarly Daycamp
Summer 2005

Volunteer: Implicated in student affairs
I managed publicity for the fashion show.
Valleyfield College
Oct. 2003

The responsible for the yearbook
Atwater High School
2001-2002

Skills: Certificate of "RC sitters"
Good with langages
CPR (can help with breeding problems)

Awards: Public Speaking Award
LaSalle Elementary School
1992

Hobbies:
Soccer, drawing, panting

BLUEPRINT FOR JOB RÉSUMÉ

Use the Blueprint to check if your job résumé covers all of the requirements in the left-hand column. Write notes for your résumé in the right-hand column.

BLUEPRINT	
PERSONAL DATA Name Address City, State Postal Code (Zip Code) Daytime telephone number (cell or pager) E-mail address	
Position applied for (or optional: job objective)	
Education (start with most recent schools). For college students, the category of *education* will usually come before *experience*. Include graduation date, degree or program, school.	
Experience (start with most recent jobs). Include period of employment, job description, employer, town/city.	

Include other relevant experience or skills.	
• Related courses/training • Volunteer work • Computer skills • Memberships in organizations or associations • Extracurricular activities • Outstanding skills or achievements • Other languages you can speak or read	
References: not really needed until you get an interview.	

Workshop

CREATE YOUR OWN JOB RÉSUMÉ

A job résumé is an advertisement in which you sell yourself. Make your résumé attractive and easy to read. Show the benefits that you can offer an employer. Without bragging or lying, you should not be modest. Project a positive feeling.

Many companies scan résumés or use a database to find key words on an electronic version. Here are some key nouns that many organizations find relevant:

reliability	software	communication skills
speed	training	problem solving
accuracy	organizational skills	responsibility
award	writing skills	

Here are three steps to follow as you write your résumé:

Step One: What defines you?

Understand what each of these adjectives means. Choose five adjectives that apply to you or your working style.

accommodating	diligent	outgoing
accurate	eager	outstanding
adaptable	efficient	perceptive
ambitious	enthusiastic	persevering
analytical	fluent	pleasant
artistic	forthright	practical
attentive	friendly	precise
bilingual	hard-working	punctual
bold	helpful	reliable
calm	honest	resourceful
capable	imaginative	respectful
careful	independent	responsible
cheerful	intelligent	self-assured
competent	keen	self-confident
confident	kind	sincere
considerate	level-headed	sociable
cooperative	likeable	straightforward
courageous	mature	tactful
creative	meticulous	thorough
dedicated	observant	trustworthy
dependable	optimistic	willing
determined	orderly	
devoted	organized	

Step Two: What kind of job do you want?

State the title of the job you want. If no particular job is open, state what you hope to learn by working for a company. Here is a list of common part-time or summer jobs for which students might apply.

babysitter	delivery driver	salesperson
bank teller	gas station attendant	ski instructor
busboy	gymnastics coach	swimming instructor
car washer	landscaper	telemarketer
camp counselor	lifeguard	telephone operator
cashier	messenger	tourist guide
clerk	mover	tree planter
construction worker	painter	tutor
data entry clerk	receptionist	waiter / waitress
daycare worker	sales representative	

Step Three: How can your skills, knowledge and past experience meet the needs of the employer?

The reader of your résumé may ask, "What can this candidate do for me that others cannot?" Think of any work you might have done, including volunteer work or extra-curricular activities at school, that shows how you are willing and able to do things. Use the list to find five action verbs that describe skills you have already demonstrated.

achieved	handled complaints	promoted
administered	hired	provided
answered questions	identified	purchased
arranged	implemented	recorded
assembled	improved	recovered
assessed	increased	reduced
balanced	installed	repaired
budgeted	interviewed	represented
built	investigated	researched
coached	maintained	selected
compiled	managed	sold
completed	met deadlines	served
conducted	obtained	solved
controlled	organized	sorted
coordinated	ordered	supervised
delivered	oversaw	supplied
developed	planned	taught
devised	prepared	trained
displayed	processed	updated
drafted	produced	wrote
founded	programmed	

Step Four: Here is a list of extra-curricular activities, awards, and certificates that may be relevant to you. See if you are aware of the correct terms that describe them.

American Red Cross Babysitter's Training Certificate	Girl Scout leader
American Red Cross First Aid Certificate	Peer tutoring
American Red Cross CPR (Cardio-Pulmonary Resuscitation) Certificate	Playing a musical instrument
	School plays
American Red Cross Lifeguarding Certificate	Special projects at school (yearbook, school paper, graduation activities)
Art shows	Sports teams, team captain, All-Star
Coaching Certificate	Student council
Commercial driver's license	Summer courses or programs
Community service	Training sessions
Dance concerts	Traveling

Now choose the relevant information from Steps One to Four and write a first draft of your résumé. Compare it to the Blueprint to check if you have included all the requirements.

REPORT FORMAT

A good report must be reader friendly. It has to be clear and coherent. On the job or in academic writing, several types of reports exist. They may range from simple accident reports, to college research papers, from business reports for an employer to papers commissioned by the government. Companies, colleges and universities may insist on a format that you must follow. Yet, no matter what kind of report you have to produce, most reports answer the basic questions of *who, what, when, where, why* and *how*. The following sections describe a few ways to organize a clear and coherent report.

Here is a short example of the way an academic or work-related report might look. Since this report is short, an abstract is not needed.

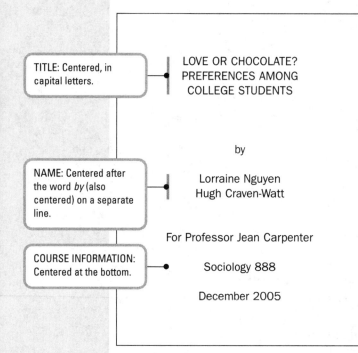

TITLE: Centered, in capital letters.

LOVE OR CHOCOLATE?
PREFERENCES AMONG
COLLEGE STUDENTS

by

NAME: Centered after the word *by* (also centered) on a separate line.

Lorraine Nguyen
Hugh Craven-Watt

For Professor Jean Carpenter

COURSE INFORMATION: Centered at the bottom.

Sociology 888

December 2005

Introduction

College students often aim to experience passion, yet passion does not mean the same thing to every person. As part of undergraduate research in the Department of Sociology, our team was asked to determine which passion is more difficult to live without for college students: the absence of love or the lack of chocolate. We wanted to find out which passion students could do without for a year.

Method

We did a survey in which we asked students to decide what would be more difficult: spending the next year without dating anyone or without eating chocolate even once. For comparison purposes, we also included questions related to sports and cars.

The survey was conducted at nine colleges, three in Quebec, four in Ontario, and two in British Columbia. We surveyed 923 undergraduate students who are working towards a bachelor's degree, 478 of whom were women. About one-third of the women said they were currently dating someone while half the men said they were. All were between the ages of 18 and 23.

Page 2

Data and Results

Results show that about two-thirds of college women said they would miss chocolate more than dating. About 12 percent of the men chose chocolate over dating. Hockey also seemed more important than getting a date, as 48 percent of the men surveyed said a year without hockey would be extremely difficult to go through.

Just over half of Quebec women currently without a boyfriend put chocolate before dates. What is interesting to note, however, is that 92 percent of those currently dating put chocolate first.

One-third of the women respondents in British Columbia said they were allergic to chocolate and could live a lifetime without eating any. The men in British Columbia cared less about hockey than students in the other provinces; less than 10 percent said they would miss hockey. One-third of them, however, would find not having a car more difficult than not having a girlfriend. The proportions are reversed for gay men: two-thirds prefer dating to car owning.

Page 3

When asked to explain why chocolate is high on their priority lists, a large number of people said chocolate could give them an energy boost at the end of a stressful day, while having to please someone might mean extra work.

Discussion / Conclusion

The results we obtained do not surprise us at all, first because good chocolate is easier to find than the right person, and secondly because chocolate is a passion that pleases you whenever you feel like having it, thus giving you complete control over the situation. Being in a relationship, however, means that you must give something to the relationship if you are going to get something out of it.

COVER PAGE

The cover page should be simple. See the model above.

Unless you formally present it in speaking to someone, do not write:

⊗ ~~Presented to~~

ABSTRACT OR SUMMARY

Many longer formal reports begin with an abstract or summary. Professionals need to know the subject and conclusions of a report, even if they are not going to read the entire document.

In the abstract or summary, you state all the central information found in the report. Include essential facts, interpretations and recommendations. The abstract or summary section must tell the reader every important feature of the report so that the reader does not have to read it in full.

Model Summary

FACTS/SITUATION

This report was written following [a request from the administration of Enki-Dupal School][to determine whether video games should be installed on the school's computers.][Our school presently has no video games on its computers.] However, a survey of recent research has shown that video games can help some autistic children relate to the world. [Interviews were conducted with the school's speech therapist and with eight parents of autistic children.][They were unanimous in saying that computers could have a positive contribution.][We conclude that using video games might improve the rapport autistic pupils have with our school's speech therapist.][We recommend that our school install video games on five computers on an experimental basis.]

METHODOLOGY

KEY RESULTS

CONCLUSION

RECOMMENDATION

Here are elements that can help you to check to see if you have included enough information in your abstract. The right-hand column proposes standard expressions that can help you get your message across effectively.

FACT / CURRENT SITUATION	SUGGESTIONS
BACKGROUND, CONTEXT	Previous studies show / Prior research indicates / However, recent research has shown / Statistics for ... These (results / differences ...) suggest / This raises questions about ...
WHAT	Our study / This report (examines / compares)...
METHODOLOGY	Data were obtained ...
KEY RESULTS OR KEY STATISTICS	
CONCLUSION	These / Our results suggest that ... may ... / This report concludes ...
RECOMMENDATIONS	We make *X* recommendations. First ...

INTRODUCTION

The introduction section provides background information and tells the larger context behind the report. State your purpose (*why*), method (*how*), and other useful aspects (*for whom?*). Present the questions or main points covered in the report and indicate how they will be presented.

While the summary *describes and gives information*, the introduction *prepares* the reader for the information; it does not go into a lot of detail. For example:

New laser technologies have opened possibilities for growth in eye clinics. Following two years of zero growth in the number of patients, the optometrists who own the Moncton Paired-Eyes Center asked our research group to evaluate the possibility of adding a laser correction surgery center to the clinic. Our work included looking for possible partnerships with a competent ophthalmologist who would perform surgical procedures and obtaining quotes for the cost of lasers. Based on these costs, we then surveyed the population to see the level of acceptance of the procedure. This allowed us to determine the potential profitability of a new laser surgery center in Moncton. This report first presents the current costs of laser technologies, then considers the types of partnerships and the distribution of costs / profits in similar ventures. Next, the report assesses the long-term profitability given the target population and potential competition. Finally, we present our recommendations.

BODY

The body section of the report presents facts, activities, and relevant data. Be sure to use concrete details with facts and examples.

The body is divided into paragraphs.

Model Body Paragraphs

Here is an example of body paragraphs taken from an accident report describing how a plane passenger was injured.

CAUSE OF ACCIDENT
The actions of the pilots and crew in the cockpit reportedly followed this sequence. First, during the flight, the captain left the cockpit to take a rest in the main cabin. His seat was then taken by the reserve first officer who replaced him. When a flight attendant brought in a box containing beverages for the flight crew, the reserve first officer asked her to place the box on the footrest of the center seat. As she had difficulty doing this, the reserve first officer became aware that the first officer's seat was blocking the way. The reserve first officer activated the horizontal movement switch for the first officer's seat, moving it forward. The first officer did not notice what the reserve first officer was doing. Since his legs were crossed when the seat moved forward, they pushed the plane's control column forward. As a result, the autopilot system was disconnected. The aircraft then responded to the forward control column motion and pitched down suddenly, resulting in injuries to passengers and crew. The first officer was able to take manual control, end the nose-dive and return the aircraft to level flight.

> **Usage Hint:**
> Note the common use of the past tense in the description of events.

FLIGHT DATA RECORDER INFORMATION
The digital flight data recorder provides specific details about the accident. Thomas R. Jacky, Aerospace Engineer, Washington, D.C., was asked to complete the readout and evaluation of the recorder from aircraft N1752K. His reading indicated that at the time of the accident the aircraft had been flying at an altitude of 33,000 feet (10,150 m), on a heading of 159 degrees, and at a position of 20.58 degrees north and 78.50 degrees west. The plane lost about 800 feet (245 m) of altitude during the nose-dive, and the passengers were exposed to a minimum force of –0.37 Gs and a maximum of +1.85 Gs.

MEDICAL INFORMATION
The altitude deviation resulted in one passenger suffering a serious internal injury and one flight attendant receiving a rib injury. Other injuries reported by the rest of the passengers and flight attendants include minor cuts, contusions and strain injuries.[1]

MORE HELP? Each paragraph should offer a new idea. See Paragraph, p. 68. The idea appears in the topic sentence. See Topic Sentence, p. 73. The topic sentence is usually the first sentence of the paragraph. Support the ideas with facts, statistics, and references to significant studies. See Support, p. 76.

---

1. Adapted from http://www.aviationnewsweb.com/aviation1/unusual.htm Downloaded 24 July, 2002.

HEADINGS

Reports usually contain headings that identify their sections and subsections. Good headings, just like the subject lines in e-mail, help the reader choose whether or not to read the paragraphs under the heading. To create a meaningful heading, find the key words that indicate what the paragraph is about and use them to guide the reader to your major ideas.

MORE HELP? See Noun-Modifying-Noun, p. 141.

Example 1: Headings in Scientific-Style Reports

TO MEET THE READERS' EXPECTATIONS:	SCIENTIFIC STYLE REPORTS usually contain the following headings.	EXAMPLE: MALE SHOPPERS[2]
Give a summary of your report so that readers can decide if they want to read it.	ABSTRACT	Abstract
Give some background and announce what your report contains.	INTRODUCTION	Introduction Prior Research
State what items you used or how you conducted the study.	MATERIALS AND METHODS	Methodology • Classification of Households • Dependent Variable • Hypothesis Testing
Give the results you obtained.	DATA AND RESULTS	Results • Demographic Contrasts • Shopping Behavior • Response to Promotions
Offer your interpretation of your results.	DISCUSSION/CONCLUSIONS	Discussion and Conclusions
List the works you have mentioned in your text. See Referencing, p. 83.	REFERENCES or WORKS CITED	References

---

2. "A Comparison of the Responsiveness of Male Shoppers Versus Female Shoppers to Sales Promotions." Brenda S. Sonner (TSUM), Gail Ayala (University of Georgia), Richard Mizerski (Griffith University). http://www.sbaer.uca.edu/docs/proceedingsII/95swa076.htm Downloaded 3 September, 2002.

Example 2: Headings in Business-Style or Academic Reports

BUSINESS-STYLE or ACADEMIC REPORTS often cover the following:	EXAMPLE: ACCIDENT REPORT	EXAMPLE: ARTIFICIAL INTELLIGENCE
ABSTRACT OR SUMMARY (if applicable)		Summary
INTRODUCTION	Introduction	Introduction
IDEA 1	Cause of Accident	Defining Artificial Intelligence (AI)
IDEA 2	Flight Data Recorder Information	AI Limitations
IDEA 3	Medical Information	Complementing Human Intelligence
CONCLUSION	Conclusion	Conclusion
REFERENCES AND APPENDIX (if applicable)	Appendix: Transcript of Cabin Conversation	Works Cited

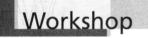

Workshop

With a partner, discuss how helpful the following headings are for the reader. Can they help you to determine what these reports are about?

REPORT 1
Traffic Statistics
Aggressive Drivers' Profile
Road Rage Victims
This report is probably about _____

REPORT 2
Children's TV Viewing Habits
Violence in Children's Programs
Television Violence and Real-life Aggression
This report is probably about _____

REPORT 3
The Risks of Genetically Engineered Foods
The Benefits of Genetically Engineered Foods
The Need for Labeling
This report is probably about _____

REPORT 4
Airport Security Measures
Plane Security Measures
Other Areas
This report is probably about _____

Check to see if you have included the necessary elements in your report. See if you can fill in the boxes in the third column. See the information boxes below to check if you have chosen appropriate grammar forms for the task. Your report will not necessarily follow the same order as the one in the Blueprint.

CHECK[3]	THE TASK	KEY WORDS FROM THE REPORT THAT SHOW THE TASK IS COVERED
1→ WHO Identify the writer (in what capacity) or team.	• Showing that you or your team can carry out what you say you will do.	
2→ WHAT Explain the task or topic that has to be covered.	• Giving a good definition/description.	
3→ WHY Give context. Justify the need for the report. Explain purpose.	• Examining the current situation or problem, often by comparing and contrasting ideas; leading to suggested improvements. Ideas that may be compared include trends, solutions, advantages, innovations, social benefits …	

1
• Check verb tenses.
• Check cause and effect transitions.

2
• Check verb tense sequence, choosing past or present.
• Check word choice (especially terminology directly related to the topic).
• Use abbreviations only if the readers are familiar with them.

3
• Check comparative forms.
• Check reported speech (verb tense sequence) when you quote sources.
• Add useful transitions.

---

3. To check grammar, please see *The Essentials of English: A Writer's Handbook*, by Ann Hogue, Pearson Education, 2003.

CHECK	THE TASK	KEY WORDS FROM THE REPORT THAT SHOW THE TASK IS COVERED
4—● HOW Explain process or methodology.	• Showing actions that should or will be undertaken.	
5—● WHEN WHERE Give time. State place. (*When* and *where* may also be included under WHY above).	• Providing specific information.	
HOW MUCH HOW MANY Give cost. Examine results.	• Using numbers that support the points.	
6—● WHAT NOW Interpret results. Recommend actions that must be taken following your report.	• Examining potential or conditional ideas. • Concluding. • Making recommendations.	

4
- Check parallelism, sentence structure, coordination.
- Make sure the passive voice is used correctly -*ing*/-*ed* (if applicable).
- Check pronoun choice.
- Check meaning of auxiliary, or helping, verbs.

5
- Check format for using numbers.
- Check use of capital letters.
- Check punctuation.
- Check dollar signs and other abbreviations.
- Check count / noncount nouns.

6
- Check conditional forms.
- Check useful auxiliary, or helping, verbs.
- Check transitions, subordination.
- Check subjunctive clauses.

VISUALS

Add any visuals, such as illustrations (drawings, photos, charts, figures), that will help readers understand the report.

CONCLUSION

Repeat useful findings that have been mentioned in the body of the report. Make suggestions that logically follow from the material you have presented. Include generalizations that can be drawn from your information. What do you want the reader to remember in a few weeks? Also mention issues that still need to be resolved or that need to be explored further in a different report.

MORE HELP? See Conclusion, p. 92.

RECOMMENDATIONS

Although recommendations are often listed within the body of the report, you can also choose the end of the text to mention suggestions or actions related to the findings of your report. For example, you can encourage readers to adopt, improve, reject, buy, or change a way of doing something.

Advanced Usage: Subjunctive Clauses

Although subjunctive clauses are not used very commonly in today's English, they still exist, in some cases, in technical and professional writing to express wishes, hopes or recommendations.

> We recommend that cell phones and pagers *be* banned from exam rooms.
> We recommend that patients not *be* allowed to place sharp objects near their beds.

After *that* clauses when a recommendation or a strong request is made, use the main form of the verb.

> It is important that the steps *be* done in order.

In formal writing, the subjunctive is also used in:

> If I *were* you ...
> I wish I *were* ...

In informal spoken English, the use of *was* instead of *were* is common:

> I wish I was an astronaut.

APPENDIX

Add any supplementary information that may be useful (for example, the questions you used in a survey, a copy of a law).

MORE HELP? If you need help with the rules for features such as abbreviations, see p. 136, noun-modifying-noun structures, p. 141, pronoun choice, p. 128, verb tenses, p. 129, and passive vs. active voice, p. 140.

ESSAY FORMAT

An *essay* is a composition that expresses the writer's personal view on a single subject. Two types are considered below, first, literary essays, then, p. 38, argumentative essays.

LITERARY ESSAYS

Some essays require a response to a piece of literature such as a short story, a passage from a long book, or an essay. The assigned questions often look like this:

> Identify a main idea in X's short story / essay / novel. Develop your essay around a thesis statement that expresses your understanding / interpretation of the short story / essay / novel. Be sure to make appropriate references to the selected text and comment on the techniques and devices used by the writer.

TECHNIQUES AND DEVICES IN LITERARY ANALYSIS

In literary analysis, you should build your analysis around commonly used *techniques* and *devices*.

BLUEPRINT FOR TECHNIQUES AND DEVICES

TECHNIQUES and DEVICES	QUESTIONS FOR ANALYSIS Here are questions you could examine to analyze the techniques and devices used by the author.	EXAMPLES Give references suggested by your teacher, or list examples found in your reading.
ANALOGY	Does the writer use the characteristics of one thing to help the reader understand something else that has similar characteristics? (See Analogy Does Not Always Work, p. 54.)	
CHARACTERIZATION	In fiction, a character is a person (or sometimes an animal with human traits). What is the contribution of a character's behavior, appearance, emotions, or moral qualities to the story?	
COMPARISON	Analysis of similarities and differences. Can your analysis be used to show the writer's attitude? Can you evaluate one piece of fiction in relation to another one? Can you look at two items you wish to analyze to discuss their respective contributions?	

TECHNIQUES and DEVICES	QUESTIONS FOR ANALYSIS Here are questions you could examine to analyze the techniques and devices used by the author.	EXAMPLES Give references suggested by your teacher, or list examples found in your reading.
CONFLICT	What produces action? Is the action the result of a person vs. another person; a person vs. himself/herself (representing a psychological, mental, emotional struggle); or a person vs. outside forces (such as environment, nature, fate)?	
CONTRAST	Often part of *comparison*. Can your analysis reveal meaningful differences?	
DESCRIPTION	Is there a detailed look at what people in the story see or feel?	
DIALOGUE	Conversations between the characters in a story. How does the dialogue contribute to the story or characterization (through the characters' level of language or tone)?	
DICTION	What techniques does the writer use to select words that affect the reader? See Connotation (p. 137) and Figures of Speech (metaphor and simile on pp. 31–32).	
EXAMPLE	Is the text developed around an illustration that helps the reader to understand an idea?	
IMAGERY	Descriptions that try to create mental images by appealing to the senses (for instance, sight). Does the writer try to create images in the mind of the reader?	

IRONY	Does the writer present something on the surface that contrasts with what he or she really thinks? Are you supposed to understand the contrary?	
LEVEL OF LANGUAGE	Can you identify formality or informality in a text? Is the language formal (polite) or informal (like standard everyday conversation)? Is slang used (special expressions, grammatical mistakes, careless pronunciation)? In dialogue, does the level of language indicate the social background of a character?	
METAPHOR	Is there a direct comparison between two things that seem quite different? (A metaphor does not, however, use *like* or *as*.)	
MOOD	What is the atmosphere (suspenseful, sad, scary ...)?	
NARRATION	Does the author tell a sequence of events or a story? Is this the author's main technique? If so, what is the author's point of view? (See below.)	
POINT OF VIEW	In fiction, what is the perspective of the narrator? For instance, do we follow the story from the view of the third-person *he/she* or the first-person *I*? Is the narrator's perspective all-knowing (omniscient) or limited? In essays, point of view refers to the opinion of the writer.	

TECHNIQUES and DEVICES	QUESTIONS FOR ANALYSIS Here are questions you could examine to analyze the techniques and devices used by the author.	EXAMPLES Give references suggested by your teacher, or list examples found in your reading.
PLOT	What is the structure of the action or thoughts in the story? (Some possibilities are exposition / description; conflict; rising action / tension; climax; falling action / relief from tension; dénouement). How important is the structure of the plot to the story you are analyzing? Does the plot follow a chronological structure? Is that structure effective?	
REPETITION	Is a word, an image, or a sound repeated for effect?	
SETTING	Where and when does the story take place? What is the importance of time and place to the story? Can the story show something about today's life?	
SIMILE	Is there a comparison in which the writer says specifically that something is "like" something else?	
SYMBOLISM	Is a concept or idea—or sometimes just a word—used to represent something else? Does it generate two meanings, literal and figurative (e.g., heart = love)? (See Connotation, p. 137, for more details.)	
THEME	What is the story about? What is the message or meaning that the author expresses in the story?	

TONE	What is the effect of the words chosen to communicate the writer's attitude (cold, friendly) or chosen to develop an emotional context (humorous, pessimistic)? (See Connotation, p. 137 and Register, p. 136.)	

BLUEPRINT FOR LITERARY ESSAYS

Use the Blueprint below to see if your essay contains the necessary elements.

While editing your text, check to see if your essay meets the requirements of the left-hand column of this chart. For each item in the left-hand column, fill in the right-hand column with key words from your essay. If your text is missing elements, add them after completing this chart.

WHAT TO CHECK	WHAT YOUR TEXT COVERS
TASK • Assigned word count • Topic	• •
COMPREHENSION AND INSIGHT • Recognition of the main idea from the selected reading. • Identification of the writing techniques used by the author. • Offering an analytical or critical interpretation of the selected reading. • Using references that show you understand what you read.	• • • •

WHAT TO CHECK	WHAT YOUR TEXT COVERS
STRUCTURE AND ORGANIZATION	
1. Introduction that states:	
• Author, genre, title of selection.	•
• Main idea of the selection you read.	•
• Thesis statement.	•
2. Unified paragraphs, each containing:	
• Topic sentence that helps prove the thesis statement.	• Idea 1:
• Support referring to reading selection (enough relevant detail).	• Support:
	• Idea 2:
	• Support:
	• Idea 3:
	• Support:
3. Conclusion that offers:	
• Review of important points, sense of closure.	•
LANGUAGE USE/EXPRESSION	
• Meaning of words.	•
• Tone.	•
• Variety in sentence structure.	•
• Transitions.	•
• Reader friendliness.	•
• Grammar, spelling, punctuation.	•

Workshop

With a partner, read the following essay (p. 36), which is a response to a piece of literature. Discuss whether the essay meets the requirements of an effective analysis. See if you can answer the following questions with information found in the text. Refer to line numbers in the text if needed.

1 Comprehension and Insight

1.1 Does the student who wrote this essay recognize the main theme in the assigned selected reading? If so, what is it? _____

1.2 Can the student identify the writing techniques used by the author? If so, what are they? _____

1.3 Is there an analytical or critical interpretation of the selected reading? If so, state.

_____

1.4 Are there references to the short story that show if the student understood the piece of literature? Is so, point out a few. (Give line number) _____

2 Structure and Organization

2.1 Is there an introduction? _____

2.2 Does the student mention the author, genre, and title of selection? If so, state.

_____

2.3 Can you identify the main idea of the selection the student read?

_____

2.4 Can you identify the thesis statement that the student will defend? If so, state.

_____

2.5 Are the paragraphs unified (all about one idea each)? _____

2.6 Does each body paragraph contain a topic sentence that helps prove the thesis statement? _____

2.7 Does the writer support each topic sentence by referring to the reading selection (and giving enough relevant details)? If so, give some line references. _____

2.8 Is there a conclusion? _____

2.9 If so, does the conclusion review some of the writer's main points? _____

2.10 Does the conclusion offer some closure? If so, state. _____

_____

3 Language Use / Expression

3.1 Are there inappropriate or incorrectly used words? If so, list.

_____

3.2 Is the tone appropriate for college writing? Give example.

_____

3.3 Is there variety in the sentence structure (a combination of simple, compound, and complex)?

Refer to line numbers to give examples: _____ _____

_____ _____ _____ _____

3.4 Are there useful transitions? If so, give examples. _____

_____

Analysis of Irwin Shaw's
The Girls in Their Summer Dresses

Men love to look at women. While state secrets are more carefully guarded than what I just revealed about the brotherhood of men, Michael Loomis's out-of-control wandering eye becomes increasingly unbearable to his wife Frances in Irwin Shaw's short story, *The Girls in Their Summer Dresses*. Shaw uses the narration of an uneventful Sunday morning to illustrate the gulf between
5 men and women. His use of dialogue shows the dramatic progression from a happy morning to the total annihilation of trust in the relationship between Frances and Michael. In using these techniques, Shaw shows us that truth may be the first casualty of love.

The author begins his narration by presenting Frances as a level-headed woman who understands that humor helps get messages across. Rather than show displeasure when Michael just looked
10 at a woman, she makes light of it.
　　"Look out," Frances said as they crossed Eighth Street. "You'll break your neck." Michael
　　laughed and Frances laughed with him. "She's not so pretty," Frances said. "Anyway, not pret-
　　ty enough to take a chance of breaking your neck." Michael laughed again. "How did you know
　　I was looking at her?" Frances cocked her head to one side and smiled at her husband under
15　　*the brim of her hat.*
Frances feels no threat to her relationship. She likes the idea of spending a quiet Sunday alone with Michael. When she asks, *"Is it a date?"* and Michael replies, *"It's a date,"* we can feel that Frances will be enjoying a perfect day.

Shaw uses Michael's renewed predatory gaze to radically alter Frances's mood. When she realizes
20 that Michael was not really listening to her plans because he was again looking at a woman, she switches from humor to anger to try to get Michael to stop. *"'You always look at other women,' Frances said. 'Everywhere. Every damned place we go.'"* Shaw widens the gap between Frances and Michael. We sense that there might have been some longing in the way Michael looked at *"the hatless girl with the dark hair."* A normal reaction would no doubt have been for Michael to apolo-

25 gize and to concoct a white lie about being more careful from now on. Michael, however, prefers to be honest and defend his actions:

> *"I look at everything. God gave me eyes and I look at women and men and subway excavations and moving pictures and the little flowers of the field. I casually inspect the universe." "You ought to see the look in your eye," Frances said, "as you casually inspect the universe on Fifth*
30 *Avenue."*

In Frances's mind, the longing looks have turned to ogling. Although Shaw does not take sides, the dialogue encourages the readers to either empathize with Frances or understand Michael's explanations.

In his narration, the author remains objective as well. He walks along with the characters as if he
35 was carrying a camera, never intruding. Yet, he shows enough that we understand the dynamics in the couple's life. While superficially, Frances now seems casual, Shaw indicates, in the way a video would, that some simmering spoils the "perfect day" she had wanted, *"her tone a good imitation of the tone she had used at breakfast."* Michael, however, understands her fears. He wants to be reassuring,

40 > *"I want to tell you something," Michael said very seriously. "I have not touched another woman. Not once. In all the five years."*
> *"All right," Frances said.*

Despite Michael's reassurances, trust is eroding. As the dialogue reveals, Frances yearns to be special but finds it impossible if Michael is totally above board,

45 > *"I try not to notice it," Frances said, "but I feel rotten inside, in my stomach, when we pass a woman and you look at her and I see that look in your eye and that's the way you looked at me the first time. (...)The same look," Frances said. "And it makes me feel bad. It makes me feel terrible."*

From humor to anger, from anger to pain, the author attributes to Frances's character a range of
50 emotions that remain equally inefficient in achieving her goal: obtaining Michael's devoted and exclusive attention.

The author's use of dialogue widens the ever-growing gap caused by Michael's honesty.

> *"I look at women (...) If I pass them on the street and I don't look at them, I'm fooling you, I'm fooling myself."*
55 > *"You look at them as though you want them," Frances said (...). "Every one of them."*

When, soon after, Michael admits that some day he might make a move on one of the women he so intently inspects, Frances can no longer deal with the truth. She begins to cry. Shaw has used a full palette of emotions to illustrate the devastating effect of the truth. Frances no longer cares about knowing,

60 > *"Stop talking about how pretty this woman is or that one. Nice eyes, nice breasts, a pretty figure, good voice." She mimicked his voice. "Keep it to yourself. I am not interested."*

If love is to have any chance, the truth must back off. Truth has become a casualty of love.

Deficient truth-management skills can destroy love. Will Michael be compounding the problem if he stays away from the truth? In the last sentence, Shaw abandons his objective-narrator point of
65 view to conclude inside Michael's mind,

> *She got up from the table and walked across the room toward the telephone. Michael watched her walk, thinking what a pretty gal, what nice legs.*

Yet, no matter how much the reader knows that this is a genuine thought, that Frances finally has Michael's devoted attention, she is not going to find out because some truths are better left
70 unsaid. (942 words)

An *argumentative essay* defends a thesis—a debatable idea. To produce a good argumentative essay, write as if the reader disagrees with you. Use facts and arguments to convince the reader that your view is right.

An argumentative essay is not limited to presenting facts, nor is it merely a list of your personal preferences and prejudices. In a good essay, you organize facts and logical arguments to show why your thesis is right and your opinion is justified.

The major elements needed to develop a good argumentative essay are covered in Part 2 of this book.

MORE HELP? See how to turn your topic into a Thesis Statement, p. 66. Use the Blueprint for Structure, p. 57, to develop your essay. For a model essay, see pp. 55-56.

Workshop

With a partner, take a position on the following questions. Discuss the points you would include in an argumentative essay.

- Should people over age seventy be allowed to drive a car?

- When people wear uniforms, do they communicate better with others?

- Given the complexity of governments today, should politicians have at least a master's degree?

- Is figure skating a sport?

- Should we ban car commercials that encourage speeding?

- Based on statistical averages, should insurance companies be allowed to charge young drivers more for insurance?

- Should universities look at more than grades when accepting or rejecting students' applications?

- Should parents be required to take parenting classes?

PART 2
COHERENCE

Content

Relevance
Logic
Accuracy
Effectiveness

Structure

Introductory Elements
Thesis Statement
Paragraph
Topic Sentence
Support
Referencing
Transitions
Conclusion
Organization

Part 2 examines how to **connect content and structure.** You will get help in checking whether your text is coherent. **Coherence** means that a text has both **relevant content** and **appropriate structure.**

Relevant content means that you choose ideas that are useful in covering the task and effective in leading to a logical conclusion. The reader can easily see how the ideas can be connected to the context of your writing task.

Appropriate structure means that the reader can easily find your introductory elements, body paragraphs and a conclusion that gives a sense of closure. Each of these parts relates to the other parts.

CONTENT

In work-related or academic tasks, you must choose content that is relevant for the task. To help you keep only appropriate ideas, this section of the book will tell you how to choose content that is relevant. In addition, it will examine potential problems you might have with the focus, accuracy, and effectiveness of your ideas.

Relevance

If comments from your instructor or classmates tell you to focus on RELEVANCE, use this section to check the following:

Can each main idea be developed and analyzed?
Does each main idea contribute to task, topic and purpose?

Coherence starts with **relevant content**: all the ideas that you choose are useful. In academic or work-related writing, an idea is useful when:

• the idea can be developed;

• the idea contributes to task and purpose;

• the idea can be logically connected to the main focus or topic of the text.

Readers expect to learn something new or at least to see facts organized in a way that gives a new view of a problem, case or situation. Are you presenting information or a view that your audience is not already familiar with? To be able to contribute a fresh angle, avoid stating very general opinions or very ordinary facts.

Compare these views on the topic of extensive use of plastic surgery:

⊗ I think everybody has to look different.

⧁ Plastic surgery has given rise to a whole generation of faces that cannot smile.

Compare the interest level in the facts below:

⊗ All cows look different.

⧁ Cloned Holstein cows show patterns of black spots that are slightly different from those of the original cow.

KEEP ONLY IDEAS THAT CAN BE DEVELOPED

In technical and professional writing, and in good academic writing, here is how you can recognize a solid **main idea**:

A MAIN IDEA IS SOMETHING YOU CAN SAY MORE ABOUT.

Look at the sentence below:

⊗ When you play basketball, you have to run.

Just stating a general truth does not lead to a serious analysis. Your readers probably already agree with you so they might not feel they have to read the rest of your paragraph.

Now compare the above sentence to the next one:

>> Many positive effects can be noted among students who play sports.

The reader will now expect the writer to give examples and an analysis of this statement.

A MAIN IDEA IS SOMETHING THAT IS SERIOUS ENOUGH TO BE ANALYZED.

Compare the following two statements. You will see that the first is a personal statement that does not lead to analysis. The second could lead to an analysis of the process of training for a particular sport:

⊗ I want to make the track team because it would be nice.

>> The top runners on college track teams follow a strict training regimen.

A solid idea is rarely a personal statement. With a solid idea, you can do one or more of the following:

- Look at the consequences (cause and effect).

- Compare the idea to something else.

- Explain the idea in greater detail.

- Explain why it can be classified in a certain category.

A GOOD MAIN IDEA ALLOWS YOU TO BACK UP YOUR WRITING WITH SOURCES OTHER THAN YOUR PERSONAL EXPERIENCE.

The idea can be supported with facts or references. For example, you can quote studies, statistics, or experts.

Model Main Idea

The following paragraph examines the development of musical tastes:

[We develop our musical tastes over a predictable period of our lives.] [According to many researchers in neurobiology, there is a window, roughly from the ages of eleven to sixteen, where people's longest-lasting musical tastes will set in.] [That corresponds to a time when young people feel that their parents are becoming less important for their survival.] New social networks are being developed with friends. [Through sharing musical tastes, teenagers form new bonds that they will rely on in subsequent years.] [These bonds can be so strong that music therapists working in nursing homes often report that ninety-year-olds laugh at the musical tastes of eighty-year-olds. Conversely, the eighty-year-olds consider that the songs enjoyed by the ninety-year-olds are old-fashioned.]

MAIN IDEA

Reference to external studies

Fact

Fact

Fact

Workshop

In each of the sentence pairs below, identify the idea that is more relevant in academic writing. Discuss with a partner.

1.1 We live in a world where there are a lot of diseases.

1.2 Many diseases in Third World countries can be prevented by proper treatment of drinking water.

2.1 We know that anorexia happens a lot.

2.2 Anorexics can be better treated with therapy than with drugs.

3.1 Heather, as everybody knows, owns an intelligent dog.

3.2 The human characteristics that the writer has attributed to the dog presume an ironic attitude towards the intelligence of dogs.

4.1 The negative effects that cars have on the environment outweigh the benefits of driving.

4.2 Cars pollute the environment.

5.1 Chess is a pretty difficult game for children to learn.

5.2 Teaching chess to children is an effective way to develop the brain.

6.1 Mordecai Richler knew Montreal well, given that he was born there.

6.2 In Mordecai Richler's novel, the closer to his dreams Duddy Kravitz gets, the less he cares about the people who surround him.

MORE HELP? See Topic Sentence, p. 73, for more on paragraph topics and controlling ideas. See Support, p. 76, for more on choosing solid support.

CHOOSE IDEAS RELATED TO TASK, PURPOSE AND TOPIC

Once you have retained ideas that can be developed, determine if each idea helps with your **task** and **purpose**, and connects to the **topic**. The task is **what you have to do**. The purpose is **why** you have to do it.

» I was asked to compare two proposals and make a recommendation (TASK) to help you decide which group should get the contract (PURPOSE).

» Our engineering firm was asked to measure the level of soil contamination at the gas station site (TASK) to decide whether a major clean-up needs to be done or whether the gas station can be reopened (PURPOSE).

Make sure that your ideas are all about the **topic** of your text. Ask yourself:

• What is my topic? (e.g., The ecological role of hunting)

• Is every idea or passage about my topic?

Compare these two ideas to see why one sticks to the topic of the ecological role of hunting and the other does not:

» Not enough predators are present in the region to control the deer population. (role of hunting: some form of population control).

⊗ There will always be deer meat available. (Not connected to ecological role of hunting.)

Problem probe

Discuss the following definition in which the writers were asked to give a definition of *mother* (TASK) to help decide whose name can legally appear as a mother on a child's birth certificate (PURPOSE). Explain why this response does not answer the question when distinctions such as biological, surrogate or adoptive mothers are considered.

⊗ A mother should support her children every single day of their lives. And it makes a difference if a mother is a full-time worker. A real mother never leaves her children. That is the law of nature.

MORE HELP? 👓 See the assigned definition task, p. 102.

Practice

Part 1. Identify the *task* and the *purpose* in the passages below. Then, for each sentence, suggest two ideas that can be connected to the task and purpose presented in the sentence. Check your two ideas with the Blueprint to see if they work.

1.1 Our marketing company was asked to create a profile of the average visitor to the Hunter Mountain Culture Festival in order to decide which types of advertising would be most effective.

1.2 The Food and Drug Administration (FDA) was asked to define "genetically modified foods" so that regulations could be implemented.

Part 2. Look at sentences 2.1 and 2.2 below. Then, with a partner, discuss how relevant each idea in a, b and c is in connection with 2.1 or 2.2.

2.1 The administration of the college should consider the benefits of advertising in college.

> **a** Advertising supplies money to colleges.
>
> **b** Ads make students lose objectivity.
>
> **c** Students are easily manipulated.

2.2 Barbie should not be regarded as a poor role model.

> **a** She is proud of being a woman.
>
> **b** Her love of shopping is good for the economy.
>
> **c** War toys have a less negative impact on women.

ASK YOURSELF	List your **main ideas** in the column below.
What is the job you have to do (TASK)? The task is to: _____ _____ For example, in academic writing: identify techniques used by a writer; analyze; propose a definition; use references. In work-related writing: examine a problem, compare ideas; check safety; make recommendations. How can each idea in the right-hand column help fulfill the task?	• Idea 1: • Idea 2:
Why is this text written (PURPOSE)? The purpose is to: _____ _____ For example, in academic writing: to show reading comprehension; persuade (in an argumentative essay); entertain. In work-related writing: to solve a problem; obtain something (information, compensation, money). How can each idea in the right-hand column contribute to the purpose?	• Idea 3:
What is the topic (or issue)? The topic is: _____ _____ How can each idea be connected to the topic?	• Idea 4:
Keep only the ideas that work well with all three elements (task, purpose, topic). Or: Clarify the logical link the idea should have with the task, purpose and topic.	

If comments from your instructor or classmates tell you to focus on your choice of idea in terms of LOGIC, use this section to check the following:

Does each idea work in relation to the other ideas?
Is each idea useful in leading to the conclusion?

KEEP YOUR FOCUS

A reader must be able to see the connection between the ideas you retain for a text. Offer consistent perspective by keeping only:

* ideas that go together (the reader can see how they have something in common);

* ideas that are at the same level or have the same importance;

* ideas that help to show why your conclusion is right.

Problem probe

Part 1. With a partner, discuss the following sets of ideas and see if you can spot the idea that does not have the same focus as the others.

Idea 1: The globalization of markets means that many people in poor countries work very hard without improving their standards of living.

Idea 2: Brand-name clothing is often made by workers who receive only a small fraction of the price people in rich countries pay.

Idea 3: Cheap labor practices mean that many workers spend over sixty hours at work every week.

Idea 4: Child hunger is also a big problem in poor countries.

Idea 1: A lot of people are afraid of spiders.

Idea 2: Agoraphobia, the fear of public places, must not be confused with shyness.

Idea 3: Humiliating reactions often make the fears of agoraphobics worse.

Idea 4: Cures for agoraphobia include medications.

Idea 1: Athletes who are convicted wife-batterers are used as role models.

Idea 2: The criminal records of athletes, some of whom have used illegal guns or knives or have attempted murder, are often overlooked.

Idea 3: We must remember that records are set to be broken.

Idea 4: Almost every athlete who gets caught in a drug test is glorified with giant news headlines quoting him or her as saying, "It was the vitamins / cough syrup / food supplements that I forgot to ask my doctor about."

Part 2. The writer of the text below seems to have lost his or her focus. Why might the conclusion surprise the reader? Look at the topic sentences and discuss what the logical conclusion should be.

Parents should not give their children hyphenated last names like Davis-Lalumière.

First, hyphenated last names are not practical because many documents don't provide enough space to write the name in full.

Many people with hyphenated last names often use just one of the last names anyway so teachers never find the names in correct alphabetical order.

Finally, there are other alternatives to hyphenated last names including choosing either parent's last name or creating a new last name.

Conclusion: In short, it is nice to be able to choose, and parents will probably keep giving children hyphenated last names.

Pay attention to other problems with logic listed below. These are common examples of cases where the writers seem to have lost their train of thought.

CONTRADICTION

Problems in logic may be caused by contradictions.

⊗ I read your comments on toxicology very carefully and found them very interesting. You caught my attention because your work needs some improvements and clarifications.

Discussion: Did the writer find this interesting because some improvements were needed?

⊗ A sport is an activity that should be for everybody.

Discussion: Are all sports for everybody? Should grandmothers play football? Is every activity that is for everybody a sport?

LACK OF NEW INFORMATION

When you lead the reader to expect new information, logic dictates that you should introduce new information. Make sure you include a new idea.

Problem probe

With a partner, discuss the problems in the sentences below and propose an improved sentence.

1 First, we must ask ourselves who was surveyed, and second, who was chosen to answer the questions. _____

_____

2 To give a big contract to an athlete is synonymous with money. _____

_____

3 The problem with exams is that they force students to memorize but we prefer to study things we can remember. _____

_____

DISCONNECTED COMMENT

In work-related or academic analyses, your opinions and comments should be based on facts. Do not add a personal comment when your task is to analyze.

Practice

Look at the first sentence in each paragraph below. Then, cross out any sentence that does not use facts to support the topic sentence before it.

1 A biological mother should have the right to have her name on her baby's birth certificate. It is a sign of respect. They should all live in peace.

2 The amount of money invested in making a movie is no better than the opinion of a reviewer for predicting what viewers will like. Action is important in a movie because it is a good indication of a good film. The majority of films made in the United States are better than movies made in Sierra Leone. Good actors are people who play a role well in a movie.

3 We have to be strict about drug sales. Medications sold online can be fakes prepared by amateurs for profit. If we regulate vitamins, the government should sell non-dangerous products. Also, profits made by big companies selling these drugs are not helping our society. It is just another capitalist tactic.

CONFUSION IN CAUSE AND EFFECT RELATIONSHIPS

Logic might need to be improved when you look at cause and effect relationships.

⊗ The patient was sick because he had a fever.

In this example, *fever* shows that the person is sick. It is not the cause.

Discuss: Is the cause and effect relationship immediately apparent in the sentences below?

⊗ To reduce obesity, the government should invest in food.

≫ The patient was sick because of food poisoning.

CONFUSION BETWEEN CORRELATION AND CAUSE

Correlation shows that two things are often found together. Their relationship, however, does not mean that one causes the other.

Discuss the problems in the sentences below.

⊗ Because the birds of spring have arrived, we will eat maple syrup on snow soon.

⊗ The writer, Ms. Chang, knows a lot about Japan because she grew up in China.

⊗ Large groups of people cause violence to occur.

JUMPING TO CONCLUSIONS

Before you can convince a reader, you must make sure that your ideas have a clear cause and effect connection. Do not make the reader think you are jumping to conclusions. Show why something causes something else.

 **MORE HELP?** See Transitions, p. 85.

⊗ Snowboarding is very popular. As a result, there are conflicts with skiers.

Although we understand the general idea, it is not immediately clear that popularity is the cause of conflicts.

The following two examples illustrate the same type of lack of logic. See what happens when we try to transpose the reasoning.

⊗ Horseback riding is very popular. As a result, there are conflicts with car drivers.

⊗ Movies are very popular. As a result, there are conflicts with TV viewers.

Discuss: Is the word *because* appropriate here?

⊗ We feel this is safe because it has been used for a long time.

Hint: Try replacing the word *this* by smoking or fire.

If comments from your instructor or classmates tell you to focus on your choice of idea in terms of ACCURACY, use this section to check the following:

Is each idea accurate?

CHECK ACCURACY

Don't make the reader think "This isn't true." Otherwise, you run the risk of losing your credibility. The reader might not trust anything you write.

Problem probe

Discuss the problems with these statements.

Example:

⊗ A mother is someone or something who has biological links with a baby.

Discussion: The above definition of mother can apply to fathers and other relatives as well. As for the word *something,* the writer probably did not re-read the text.

1 In the past five years, the deer population has doubled in eastern cities.

2 The society went through a lot of changes in the last century. There have been the wheel, electricity, the whole computer world, and many more inventions.

3 Since the beginning of time, humans have constantly been trying to improve technology.

4 Since the creation of humans, animals have always been eaten. But during the last few years, scientists at the U.S. Food and Drug Administration have discovered diseases in the meat that we are eating.

5 It is a good idea to focus on teens because teens are the future population.

6 The police are the only organized group that can make laws in the U.S.

Idea 4: How much

    A. Determining cost of hiring policy

        1. Personnel department

        2. Finance department

Conclusion

    A. Essential contribution of every age group

        1. Better age range needed

        2. Makes for better organization

    B. Need to hire inexperienced people

Practice

Complete the outline by developing the third main point and adding a conclusion below.

THESIS STATEMENT: Cheating must be accepted as a fact of life

Introduction

I. First main point: Cheating in College

    A. First sub-point: Students

        1. Further subdivision: Papers are often plagiarized.

            a) Yet further subdivision: Easy to get on the Internet.

            b) On sale at the cafeteria.

        2. Exams

            a) Exams are easy to buy.

            b) Codes are used during multiple choice tests.

            c) Students hide their notes during exams.

    B. Second sub-point: Professors

        1. Infringe copyright laws in handouts.

        2. Borrow ideas without reference.

            a) Take ideas from student papers.

            b) Take ideas from colleagues.

II. Second main point: Cheating on Taxes

    A. Working under the table

        1. Barter among white-collar employees and owners of small businesses.

        2. Construction workers take cash and do not declare income.

    B. Black market

        1. Smuggling

            a) Cigarettes

            b) Alcohol

            c) Drugs

Effectiveness

If comments from your instructor or classmates tell you to focus on your choice of idea in terms of EFFECTIVENESS, use this section to check the following:

Is each main idea effective in leading to and showing why your conclusion is true?

CHOOSE EFFECTIVE IDEAS

Work-related or academic texts must contain effective ideas. This usually means using enough facts and references to make the reader agree that what you wrote can be trusted.

MORE HELP? 👓 See Support, p. 76, for more on supporting your ideas.

Check the following sections. They show why a reader might think your text is not effective.

SOURCE NOT CREDIBLE

Which source would be more convincing in work-related or academic writing?

⊗ My aunt told me ...
OR
≫ A study by a team of researchers in medicine at Harvard indicates ...

⊗ The car salesman explained to us that gas consumption is now lower.
OR
≫ Professor Wong explained the process through which engines now consume less gas.

Be extremely careful when quoting sources from the Internet to make sure that the source can be trusted.

OPINION, CLAIM VS. FACT

Make sure you can discriminate between **claims** and **facts** when you use sources. Generally, relevant and effective evidence consists of facts.

A *fact* is something that is admitted as true because it can be checked and proven. The following sentence is a fact:

In 1952 Jonas Salk developed a vaccine against polio.

A *claim* is something that some people say is true or is a fact, but they might not be able to offer proof. As a result, other people might not believe the claim. The following sentence contains a claim:

The chances of meeting the right person are higher if we use Internet dating.

Of course, a claim can become a fact if it can be proven true.

An **opinion** is what a person believes, but that belief is not necessarily shared by other people.

> The artistic merit of the figure skater's performance was certainly worth 4.8, not 4.6.

> Marrying a rich older person is a good way to get through college.

An **interpretation** is how a situation, a law, or the results of a study are explained. Different people may have different interpretations of the same situation or results.

> Sales have been slow because our new product was not marketed properly.

> Sales have been slow because most of our customers have to deal with budget cuts.

> Sales have been slow because customers know that our first version did not work properly.

Practice

What ideas are not facts? Separate facts from opinions in the following passages by circling the elements that are not facts.

1 Anne Gunter, the daughter of Brian Gunter, lived in North Moreton, a small English village approximately nineteen kilometres from Oxford. In the summer of 1604, when she was about twenty, she fell ill. Doctors were called, but they were unable to diagnose the problem. They suggested, however, that the causes might be supernatural.

Anne was showing all the classic symptoms of demonic possession, or the more serious forms of witchcraft-induced illness. She was foaming at the mouth, vomiting and went into violent fits and contortions.[1]

2 Endometriosis, the painful condition that can cause infertility and afflicts millions of women, may be triggered by wearing tight clothing during teenage years.

A leading medical scientist has uncovered evidence that the pressure caused by wearing tight clothes can lead to a build-up of cells from the womb's lining elsewhere in the body—the cause of endometriosis.[2]

3 On June 30, 1908, a meteoroid exploded about five kilometres above the Earth over the Tunguska River in Central Siberia. That night, people, five thousand kilometres away in London, could read newspapers by the glow of day.

Villagers, hundreds of kilometres from the point of impact, reported fierce winds and scorching heat, a fireball brighter than the sun, a huge cloud of black smoke, a forked tongue of flame, and a loud boom like cannon fire. They fled in panic. Some wept for the end of the world.

For all its fury, the Tunguska event may be only one small sample of a long history of close encounters with the debris left by a great disintegrating comet.[3]

1. Sharpe, James (1999, Nov. 24). *National Post*, p. A17.
2. Mathews, Robert (1999, Nov. 24). *National Post*, p. A17.
3. Boisseau, Peter (1998, Nov. 12). *National Post*, p. A17.

PART 123
EFFECTIVENESS

INSUFFICIENT DATA

To include enough information you should consider the following:

- Before you write your conclusion, be sure that your text offers enough data or information to convince your reader. This means two or three solid main ideas.

  ⊗ In the previous paragraph I mentioned how important it is to say no to your friends when you have to work. Now for my third point, I would like to repeat that it is important because you cannot always be with your friends when you have a part-time job and go to school.

- Including enough information means that you should put in what is needed to help the reader judge if your points are credible.

  ⊗ Two of three people said that ...
  Who are these people?

  ⊗ We looked at the problem and we all agree that the solution we retained is much better. Better than what? Better for what?

- As well, using only one relevant element of support is not enough to be effective. Check every paragraph and see if you have at least two elements of support in each. See Support, p. 76.

ANECDOTE VS. ANALYSIS

Anecdotes and personal stories may make your text more interesting, but you cannot generalize from them. Anecdotes can be effective, for example, in news items where they might make people want to react to a situation. In essays, they might be used to entertain the reader with an unusual story that leads into the main point.

Before you use an anecdotal fact or idea to prove a point in academic or work-related writing, ask yourself "Can I use this particular case or example to generalize and apply my idea to a larger group?"

Consider the following situation: Six hundred Japanese children were rushed to hospitals after brilliantly flashing scenes in *Pokemon* caused convulsions and nausea. Can you see which statement is anecdotal?

a   A writer specializing in animation and comic books, Toshio Okada, said that Japanese cartoons require too much intense concentration.

b   Brain researchers say the show might have affected children who had an undiagnosed epileptic problem, as a small percentage of the population is sensitive to flashes of light.

Using an anecdote might make people question where you took your facts if the details of an anecdote change over time. Note the differences in the re-telling of the Picasso anecdote below. Do the changes affect credibility?

a Picasso was once accosted on a train by a stranger who recognized him. The stranger complained: Why couldn't he draw pictures of people the way they actually were? Why did he have to distort the way people looked? Picasso then asked the man to show him pictures of his family. After gazing at the snapshot, Picasso replied, "Oh, is your wife really that small and flat?" To Picasso, any picture, no matter how "realistic," depended on the perspective of the observer.[4]

b Years ago, the legendary photographer Alfred Stieglitz reportedly told Pablo Picasso, "I don't understand your paintings. They don't look like anything." With that he showed the artist a photograph of his wife, the painter Georgia O'Keefe. "This is my wife," he continued. "This is exactly what she looks like." Picasso looked at the snapshot, then replied politely, "Small, isn't she?"[5]

Problem probe

Discuss the relevance and effectiveness of the ideas below.

Background: the writers' task was to make a funding decision based on the presentation of budgets.

1 First, the team was very comfortable in presenting this project. The other team, which presented on government regulation of vitamins, was not so confident about asking for money for their project.

2 Another aspect I considered is the realistic cost. One team gave us a detailed budget. We know where the money goes, to which person. The second team was not as good because their poster was smaller.

3 As you both presented processes related to a social problem, I would like to examine which solution is easier to develop based on the budgets you submitted, yours or Ms. Kleen's. First, I thought your budget was weaker because of the intonation of your voice. You only read the points.

COLLAGE OF QUOTATIONS WITH NO ANALYSIS

References are useful if they help to show why your ideas are true. Do not use a series of quotations just because you think this will make the reader happy. Make sure that the reader thinks you have personally contributed enough originality to the text. Discuss the effectiveness of the following passage.

⊗ My research shows that art and literature are very important in our society because John F. Kennedy spoke at Harvard in 1956 and said, "If more politicians knew poetry, and more poets knew politics, I am convinced the world would be a little better place in which to live." As well, Erich Fromm said, "All great art is by its very existence in conflict with the society with which it coexists." But of course, others such as Picasso don't agree: "We all know that art is not truth. Art is a lie that makes us realize truth."

---

4. Kaku, Michio. (1994) *Hyperspace: A Scientific Odyssey Through Parallel Universes, Time Warps, and the 10th Dimension.* Anchor, p. 65.

5. Fisher, David. (1995) *How Detectives Inside the FBI's Sci-Crime Lab Have Helped Solve America's Toughest Cases.* Simon & Schuster, p. 273.

PART 1 2 3
EFFECTIVENESS

PREJUDICE OR CLICHÉ

Do not use a religious book as a reference to prove a point in academic writing. People from a different religion may not be convinced by your argument.

The fact that many people think in a certain way does not make for effective support of your view. Remember that for centuries, almost everyone would have told you the Earth was flat. Even general agreement among the population did not make the Earth flat.

Problem probe

Discuss the problems in the passages below.

1 We must encourage people to stop smoking because you cannot do to others what you don't want to do to yourself.

2 Mr. Dam gave us statistics on all the money we spend each year because of drunk people. His project to develop a pill for drunks would probably save lives, too. Another point is the amount of people who could use the product because everybody drinks. A pill for drunks could be used by numerous people.

ANALOGY DOES NOT ALWAYS WORK

An analogy is a comparison in which you say that one thing is like another. An analogy must help the reader understand better.

Problem probe

Do these analogies help readers to understand your point better? Compare and discuss.

1 Emotions are like water and we have to express these to be in good health.

2 A woman who expects a baby feels as full as a balloon about to burst.

3 Mountains float, like icebergs, upon the mantle of the Earth, with most of their mass miles below the surface.[6]

4 Think about what happens when you load a washing machine unevenly. Midway through the spin cycle, the machine starts bumping and thumping and walking across the floor, and your clothes end up in a wet messy ball. Amusement rides aren't much different, only they're a lot bigger and they've got human beings inside.[7]

5 Like many climate scientists, I will explain the random element in the weather by saying that climate is like a set of dice with some dry faces, wet faces, hot faces, cold faces and so on. The problem with global warming is that we might be loading the dice in such a way that the problem faces of the dice will turn up more often than chance would predict.

6. Jones, Steve. (2001) *Darwin's Ghost*. Ballantine, p. 199.

7. 15 Nov. 2000 http://www.saferparks.org/safety_tips

STRUCTURE

Coherence combines **relevant content** (previous section) and **appropriate structure** (below). In a work-related or academic text, the reader must be able to see a logical sequence in the development of the ideas (or arguments). Readers expect introductory elements, body paragraphs and closure. The facts and arguments should be arranged in a logical manner, with useful transitions between the ideas. This gives your text cohesion by helping to show how each part of the text relates to the other parts.

Model Essay
Elite Sports Programs Are Not For Children

The following essay is an example of effective structure developed with the Blueprint on p. 57.

BLUEPRINT	CONTENT
INTRODUCTORY ELEMENTS • Background • Purpose (in reports) / Thesis (in essays) • Announce content	Sportscasters constantly remind us of "the thrill of victory." Schools often recruit students on the basis of athletic abilities. Sports, in the public perception, are often seen as an education in themselves, paving the way to the development of well-rounded individuals. Yet, if a high school recruiter came to our house to offer my 11-year-old sister a sports scholarship, I would beg my parents to say no. Elite sports programs are not for children. The myth must be examined with some real questions. What happens when the glorification of the heroes leads to countless children being hurt physically, drained emotionally, and ashamed of their parents?
FIRST IDEA SUPPORT	First, we tend to forget that young bodies might suffer from overuse. Physical pain and sometimes disabling injuries are common. Several American studies have shown that children who undergo long hours of training, usually more than 18 hours a week before puberty, tend to have more health problems than average children. Consider growth disorder, a problem that afflicts many gymnasts. One often cited example is Olympic gymnast Dominique Moceanu who retired from competition at the age of 20. So much sport at such a young age can bring about, in addition to the growth disorder she suffered from, eating disorders and menstrual dysfunction. Before putting a child through such training, parents should consider the long-term pain that follows the fleeting gain.

Transitions

BLUEPRINT	CONTENT
SECOND IDEA SUPPORT	<u>Secondly</u>, success at all cost should never prevail over the joy of playing sports. Given that there will always be just one winner and a lot of losers, the agony of defeat has no place in children's sports. We must do a better job at reminding children that sports are just a reason to go out and be fit. Too many young athletes ride on their parents' or coaches' motivation rather than on their own. Yet, whose motivation matters more, the adults' obsession or the child's need for enjoyable leisure time? Some statistics show that by age 14, 75 percent of children have dropped out of organized sports. What is the primary reason that they offer? It's not fun. Children will suffer from anxiety when, as in most cases, they realize that they do not have the skills to meet their parents' and coaches' expectations. Parents would be better off advising their children that statistically it is far more normal not to win than to treat every loss as a tragedy.
THIRD IDEA SUPPORT	<u>Finally</u>, we commonly hear that irresponsible parents sit in the stands at arenas, yelling abuse at referees and coaches, and asking for the blood of opponents. Violent arguments between parents are commonplace in arenas, and even soccer moms get into fights. One wonders what such parents would be like if sports were not merely a game! What has been called the "Little League Parent Syndrome" can lead to extreme cases: Thomas Junta of Reading, Massachusetts, beat Michael Costin to death over their sons' hockey game. The mother of a cheerleader tried to have another cheerleader killed to guarantee her daughter a spot on the team. Beneath these extremes, there are thousands of screaming parents out there. Where are children supposed to go to hide from such an embarrassing presence? A child has no option. Yet, few children are equipped to compensate for their parents' failure.
CONCLUSION / CLOSING • Confirm • Point out what is to be remembered • Limit / Expand	No matter how rich my little sister could get if she developed into a professional athlete, I simply see too many problems in allowing children to play elite sports. I would try to convince my parents that co-operation and leadership can be learned outside of formal sports contexts. Going through "serious sports" early in life might not be beneficial after all. When sports scare away reasonable people who understand that a game is about sportsmanship and fun, who will be left to teach the love of games? When under-age opponents begin to perceive sports as war, they may as well become gang members. (645 words)

Transitions

This structure works for formats such as essays, letters and reports. Check if your structure matches the Blueprint. Indicate which part corresponds to the elements in the left-hand column.

BLUEPRINT	YOUR FINISHED PRODUCT	
	TRANSITIONS	CONTENT
INTRODUCTORY ELEMENTS • Background • Purpose (in reports)/ Thesis (in essays) • Announce content (in longer texts)		
FIRST IDEA SUPPORT		
SECOND IDEA SUPPORT		
THIRD IDEA SUPPORT		
CONCLUSION / CLOSING • Confirm • Point out what is to be remembered • Limit / Expand		

MORE HELP? For specific models of organization, please see Definitions, p. 96, Process, p. 110, Comparison, p. 103 and Cause and Effect, p. 116. See the appendix for models of letters.

Before writing a full essay or doing a presentation on an issue, outlining your ideas can help you see the structure of your main points and sub-points clearly. It can also help you check whether anything is missing from your text. A standard outline would look like this:

Introduction / background

    A. Not enough young employees in our company

    B. Hiring policy needed

Idea 1: What

    A. Hiring young, inexperienced employees essential to our company

        1. Current situation

            a) Mostly experienced workers

                – Need to pass down knowledge, ensure continuity, tradition.

            b) Some on-the-way-up, mid-thirties

                – Seem to want more time with family.

Idea 2: Why

    A. Company lacking:

        1. Young, energetic employees to complement experienced and on-the-way-up employees

        2. Creativity: more needed

            a) more creative when young

                – Science: Newton / gravity, 20s

                      Einstein / law of relativity, 26

    B. Young employees have better understanding of the world around them.

        1. Know how young people buy.

        2. Understand sources of influence among the young.

            a) new faces (example)

            b) new trends (example)

        3. Feel very comfortable with new technologies.

Idea 3: How

    A. Developing hiring policies that encourage young people to apply

    B. Setting target quotas

    C. Active recruiting in colleges and universities

    D. Promoting creativity

    E. Encouraging transfer of knowledge from experienced workers to recently hired ones

        1. Formal training sessions

        2. Job sharing prior to retirement

2. Stolen goods

3. Counterfeiting / bootlegged CDs

C. Buying goods with cash to avoid taxes

III. Cheating the Consumer

A. _____

1. _____

2. _____

B. _____

1. _____

2. _____

Conclusion

_____

_____

_____

Introductory Elements

If feedback from your instructor or classmates tells you to focus on INTRODUCTORY ELEMENTS, use this section to check the following:

> **In what context was your text written (background information)? What is the text about?**
> **Why was the text written? (task and purpose)**
> **In longer texts, have you provided a general idea of content?**

To produce a good introduction, always write as if the reader knows nothing about your text. Even when the reader is the person who has asked you to write the text, the person might not remember what the request was.

A good introduction must show what is specific to your text. Don't write an introduction that is so general that you could use it for another text and it would still work.

A good introduction offers some background information that gives a context to the reader. The introduction should clarify what the text is about and explain why the text was written.

In an introduction to longer texts, indicate how your ideas will be organized.

GIVE BACKGROUND INFORMATION OR CONTEXT

Presume that the reader knows nothing about your topic.

1 Give the context and circumstances around the writing of your text.

- Start at a point in time that is relevant to your topic or to your task.

- Start with information that is helpful to the reader.

2 Tell the reader what the text is about.

- State especially what is new, important or essential.

Examples:

Letter

Relevant point in time

Context and circumstances

What the text is about

[Last week,] [while you were away,] I attended, [at your request,] the presentation of two projects related to health problems. [One project proposed renovating a wing of our hospital and using it for highly contagious patients. The other project was related to prevention.] It requested funds for an anti-smoking campaign. I have analyzed the projects with two criteria and will explain why …

Essay

Relevant point in time

Context and circumstances

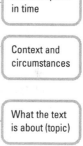

What the text is about (topic)

Discoveries in the field of medical science are in the news [every day.] [Newspaper articles and television reports seem to promise miracle cures that would make any patient impatient. Yet, the race for the perfect drug and the pressure exerted by patients who have come to expect quick fixes may hide a serious disregard for or even a lack of ethical concerns.] [Because of the moral concerns attached to the ethics of research, I will examine the current ethical guidelines used by the Faculty of Medicine.]

> **A GOOD LEAD WILL MAKE READERS INTERESTED**
>
> Few people read a text unless they think it might interest them. In *essays*, try to catch the readers' attention. In *letters* or *reports*, tell the readers why the text concerns them. Even *scientific reports*, which can be very dry, can gain from a somewhat personal context.

Workshop

Part 1. With a partner, discuss how complete the following introductions are.

- Identify the context and circumstances that led to the text.

- Find a relevant time reference.

- State the helpful information that tells the reader what the text is about.

Letter

In response to your April 4th request for an art display on Granville Island, I regret to inform you that we will not be able to let you use a public space for your project.

Report

Patients at our sleep-disorder clinic have been complaining for at least three years about the need for more details on the procedures they will undergo while spending nights here. In addition, they have requested better information about the length of their stay so that they may plan their family life better.

Essay

Drugs, corruption and bribery are words usually associated with organized crime. Since the last Olympics, however, a reader can encounter these terms in the sports pages almost as often as in police reports. Although sports promoters will tell you that there is no such thing as bad publicity when you intend to make money by packaging sports as a commercial product, the scandal in figure skating judging and the extensive use of drugs by athletes might scare away potential sponsors. Good corporate citizens will see no benefit in being associated with cheaters.

Part 2. Now consider the introductions below. Presuming the reader knows nothing in advance, discuss the problems in the passages below with a partner.

- Do you learn about the context and circumstances around the writing of the text?

- Does the introduction start at a point in time that is relevant to the topic?

- Can the reader find out what is helpful, new, important or essential?

1 I want to give you my point of view on two projects. I will compare them to give you a good idea of which project is stronger.

2 Ever since the beginning of humankind, health has been a problem.

3 In today's society, everything is related to money. And everything can be done to get money fast. Dostoyevski's *The Gambler* shows this.

4 This essay will look at a book written by a Canadian writer, Lucy Maud Montgomery. Ms. Montgomery's story is about a young orphan. We see life in the country and the relationships between people.

5 With computers, criminals do not have a face anymore. They have a nickname that is difficult to catch. So if you have a company, you have to protect yourself.

STATE TASK AND PURPOSE

In letters and reports, introductory elements should also state **what you have to do** (TASK) and why you have to do it (PURPOSE). State the task and the purpose of your text in addition to the background information you have already offered.

≫ Patients at our sleep-disorder clinic have been complaining for at least three years about the need for more details on the procedures they will undergo while spending nights here. In addition, they have requested better information about the length of their stay so that they may plan their family life better. We were asked to develop a communication strategy (TASK) to help patients understand what their stay at the clinic will involve (PURPOSE).

What do you want to accomplish by writing this text? For example:

- Were you asked to **give information**?

- Do you want to **solve a problem** by proposing a solution?

- Were you asked to **make suggestions or recommendations**?

≫ I was asked to write a letter explaining (TASK) why I should be considered for the scholarship (PURPOSE).

≫ Our firm was asked to write a feasibility study for the development of an advertising campaign (TASK) to encourage people to use alternative forms of transportation (PURPOSE).

≫ I was asked to compare two proposals and make a recommendation (TASK) to help you decide which group should get the contract (PURPOSE).

In literary analysis or in academic essays, the task is usually to **defend a thesis**. If so, write a clear thesis statement. Your purpose is then to **convince** the reader that your thesis is justified.

≫ The use of a child protagonist in Harper Lee's *To Kill a Mockingbird* and the use of a young girl in *The God of Small Things* by Arundhati Roy show the effectiveness of non-adults' points of view.

MORE HELP? See Thesis Statement, p. 65.

GIVE A GENERAL IDEA OF TEXT CONTENT

Depending on the format of your text, you may want to add a general idea of what your text contains. In short letters and reports, this is not always necessary. In a longer analysis, however, this statement would help to prepare the reader. In essays, the reader often expects you to announce the ideas you will be covering.

Examples:

Letter

In response to your request about determining priorities in the evaluation of employee performance, we have analyzed the evaluation procedures in three businesses that are similar to our own. Based on our findings, we think that two major criteria should be given top priority: quantity of work and initiative. We explain below why these two criteria would work well in our company.

Essay

After presenting background information and your thesis, you can announce what you will cover.

... We will consider three reasons why we must understand the limits of the information found in newspapers. First, we will look at journalists who recycle press releases, then we will see how short quotes prevent serious analysis, and finally we will examine how deadlines make it impossible to consider the relative importance of an event.

Although the information you include does not have to follow the order presented below, your reader should be able to find all the major elements easily. Check if your introduction matches the Blueprint. Indicate which part of your introduction corresponds to the part in the left-hand column.

Usage Hint:

In letters, check the verb tense you start with:
I was asked ...
I am writing ...

BLUEPRINT	YOUR FINISHED PRODUCT
Give background information. Place the reader in the context. What does the reader need to know about the situation?	
State what the text is about, mention your **task** (what you are doing) and **purpose** (why you are doing it). In academic essays, present the central question or thesis statement.	
In longer texts, give a general idea of content.	

Using the Blueprint above, decide with a partner which introductory elements are missing from the following introductions:

1 First, let me thank you for asking me to help. I think that technology is good in terms of job creation. Technology is the future and that's where money is. Maybe people think robots would do all the work instead of human beings but I disagree.

2 I am writing to answer your question so I am going to give you my point of view. I hope my letter will help you in this matter. First, I will look at the risks and then at the cost.

3 My name is Carla and I think you need to learn a few things about the way people buy medications. Too many use the Internet without a prescription. Let's see how it works.

MORE HELP? See Format for more on introductions in letters, p. 6, and in reports, p. 22.

Thesis Statement

If feedback from your instructor or classmates tells you to focus on THESIS STATEMENT, use this section to check the following:

Is your thesis debatable?

WORK ON YOUR THESIS STATEMENT

In a persuasive or opinion essay, your topic must become the subject of your thesis statement. A **thesis statement** is a debatable affirmation expressing an opinion, an attitude, or an original idea on the topic or on a piece of literature. Your thesis statement can be controversial. Some people will disagree with you. For example:

• The time has come to go back to single-sex schools.

• Children with learning disabilities must not be rejected by day-care centers.

• Cinderella's evil stepmother is not a myth.

In a literary analysis, a thesis statement can express your intention to demonstrate why your understanding or interpretation of a reading is justified.

≫ In *Explaining Death to the Dog*, Susan Perabo draws an analogy between the dog's failure to understand death and the main character's own inability to cope with her child's death.

PART 1 2 3
THESIS STATEMENT

A thesis statement is not a simple announcement.

⊗ This essay is about the father of a handicapped child in *The Weekend Man*.

⊗ I am going to write about a boy on a boat in *Life of Pi*.

CHARACTERISTICS OF A THESIS STATEMENT

A thesis statement has:

- only one topic (your subject) + your comment (point of view)

- at least one verb

- a focus limited enough to be developed in the assigned length (e.g., 750 words).

Compare:

Usage Hint:
To be sure that a thesis in an academic essay is debatable, use *should* in your statement.

⊗ The bad consequences of plastic surgery.

» Plastic surgery | should be | illegal .
    TOPIC   VERB   COMMENT

⊗ An interesting novel, *High Fidelity*.

» The novel, *High Fidelity*, | presents | a perfect example of men's inability to achieve maturity .
    TOPIC   VERB   COMMENT

What is the difference between a thesis statement and the topic sentence of a paragraph?

THESIS STATEMENT	TOPIC SENTENCE
A thesis statement is necessarily debatable.	A topic sentence does not have to be debatable.
A thesis statement uses many ideas in its development. It applies to the whole text or presentation.	A topic sentence applies to one paragraph only.

DEVELOPING A THESIS STATEMENT

If, for instance, you choose Plastic Surgery as a topic, you obviously have too broad a subject for a 500- or 750-word essay. You need to focus on a specific aspect of plastic surgery that you can manage within the limits. Thus, if your thesis statement is "The cost of training doctors is so high that we should ban all unnecessary plastic surgery," you are capable of analyzing studies in which the views of patients, doctors and the government are introduced. This more narrow topic will allow you to support your position and offer your own conclusion on the issue.

Example:

Topic you have in mind and need to refine: *Pollution*.

- First attempt at a thesis statement: *Noise pollution*. (Rejected: This is still too broad a topic.)

- Second attempt at a thesis statement: *Urban highways are noisy.* (Rejected: This is not an idea presented in debatable form.)

- Third attempt: *Urban highways must be built underground.* (Accepted: The statement has a clearly focused topic and a debatable opinion.)

Your essay would then state facts and statistics showing what happens to the level of decibels in cities where highways are underground. You could also discuss the social costs of the problem, financial considerations, government apathy and public reaction.

Here are ideas that need work in order to become thesis statements:

A THESIS STATEMENT MUST BE EXPRESSED IN A COMPLETE SENTENCE.

⊗ Homeopathy. (just one word, the general topic)

⊗ Violence in cities. (no verb, just a topic)

⊗ Eating disorders in Margaret Atwood's *The Edible Woman*. (sentence fragment)

A topic must be used as the subject of a full sentence. If you have not written a complete sentence, you still do not have a thesis statement.

A THESIS STATEMENT IS NOT A PERSONAL PREFERENCE.

⊗ Judo is a good activity.

⊗ *Anne of Green Gables* is a good story.

⊗ Rap music is the most interesting in the world.

The statements above express personal preferences, not a structured analysis. They might be difficult to explain with serious factual support. Someone else might use exactly the same points and support to show, for example, that badminton rather than judo is a "good" activity. In addition, the use of general words like *good, better, best* and *interesting* makes the focus hard to see as these terms mean different things to different people.

A THESIS STATEMENT IS NOT A QUESTION.

⊗ How can you cure your fear of snakes?

⊗ Does Sylvia Plath announce her suicide in her poem "Lady Lazarus"?

⊗ Why should gun control laws be tougher?

A thesis statement offers your opinion on your topic. A question does not offer your point of view.

A THESIS STATEMENT IS NOT A FACT.

⊗ Water is in short supply in the Middle East.

⊗ Dogs have bad breath.

⊗ Dr. Oliver Sacks's book is a best-seller.

Once you have stated a well-known fact, the reader can only agree with you. There is nothing left to write.

Workshop

With partners, choose one inappropriate statement from each of the four categories of problems shown on p. 67. Improve each of the four statements you choose, to turn them into acceptable thesis statements.

1 Complete sentence: _____

_____

2 Not a personal preference: _____

_____

3 Not a question: _____

_____

4 More than a fact: _____

_____

Paragraph

If feedback from your instructor or classmates tells you to focus on PARAGRAPH, use this section to check the following:

Do you need to start a new paragraph?
Are all the ideas in your paragraph related to your topic sentence?

START A NEW PARAGRAPH

Start a new paragraph for each new **main idea** or each important aspect of an idea.

First, the park that we intend to build has something to teach everyone about the environment. Children will like our miniature train that takes them on a tour where a guide explains the work that was done on the park's environment. Parents will enjoy the recycling center where the whole process of recycling is explained. As they walk through the park, the elderly will find many spots where they can sit and watch short films that explain the changes between the way things were done "back in the good old days" and what new technologies contribute to a clean environment. ⊗ The park will also create jobs because we want to give students some work experience.

Where you see the symbol ⊗, the writer needs to start a new paragraph because a new idea, job creation, is introduced. The main idea of the paragraph was that the park could *teach everyone something about the environment.*

What does *idea* mean in technical and professional writing? See Relevance, p. 40.

Problem probe

Do the passages below need to be broken into paragraphs? If so, indicate where.

1 The School Breakfast Program consists of providing balanced breakfasts to children in schools in poor districts. The project meets our first criterion, being easy to implement. We received a realistic plan for preparing and delivering the meals, supported by a detailed budget. The limited number of people needed to run the program makes it easy to manage and as such would make the School Breakfast Program easy to implement. Concerning our second criterion, effectiveness, the project would reach the schools located in the poorest districts. Hunger is indeed a problem in many poor areas. Access to breakfast would help many pupils to focus on learning rather than on their empty stomachs.

2 I attended the presentation in which you explained last week how to fight the black market. I compared your presentation with one on tax evasion to decide which one I would recommend to the task force for development. I have a couple of suggestions to give you. First, with your topic, you should have used statistics. At the end of your presentation, we did not know how important the black market should be considered in terms of government losses. Giving a definition is not enough. Second, your ideas should lead to your conclusion. We were not interested in your attitude. We were interested in how we could solve the problem. What stimulating innovations could you contribute to fighting the black market? Whose responsibility should it be? Your task was to present a way to fight the phenomenon, not just to say that it exists.

PART 1 2 3
PARAGRAPH

Do you need to start a new paragraph? Check the following.

	LIST OF INTRODUCTORY ELEMENTS
Is your introduction complete? List your introductory elements in the right-hand column. (See pp. 60-63 for help.) In your text, start a new paragraph after the last introductory element.	• Background: • Task and purpose: • Announcement of what is coming (if useful):
	LIST OF MAIN IDEAS IN TOPIC SENTENCES
Is there a new paragraph for each new idea? In the right-hand column, list the main ideas shown in your topic sentences. There should be a new paragraph for each of these ideas. If you have not done this, go back to your text and start a new paragraph for each new main idea.	1. 2. 3.

PARAGRAPH LENGTH

Try to avoid one-sentence paragraphs. Although they are common in newspaper articles, one-sentence paragraphs do not offer the support needed in technical and professional writing. In technical and professional writing, good paragraphs are made up of a **topic**

sentence (see p. 73) and **support** (see p. 76). Usually, paragraphs contain enough information when they are 75-100 words or about eight lines long. Such paragraphs make for blocks that do not appear intimidating to the reader. Paragraphs that are too long (over 200 words) will make your text seem more difficult. See where you can break down the ideas.

CHECK PARAGRAPH UNITY

A good paragraph breaks up your thinking into separate units. To show **unity**, each component of thought should focus on:

- one main idea that you express in your topic sentence

- supporting information that can be connected to that main idea.

If you cannot connect the meaning of the smaller bits of information to your main ideas, do not include the information in the paragraph.

BLUEPRINT FOR PARAGRAPH UNITY

To check paragraph unity, take a paragraph you wrote and break it down into the boxes below.

MAIN IDEA	TOPIC OF PARAGRAPH	FOCUS OF PARAGRAPH (CONTROLLING IDEA)
Break your topic sentence into topic / focus and write it in the boxes on the right.		
NEW INFORMATION		
Can you explain how each new piece of supporting information can be connected to the topic and focus above? (Adding details; giving examples, illustration; giving cause or effects; proving with facts or literary examples.) **Cross out** your sentence if there is no connection.		

MORE HELP? See Disconnected Comment, p. 47 and Accuracy, p. 49.

Workshop

Bring a variety of paragraphs to class (for instance, one you found on the Internet, one from a textbook, one from a magazine, one from a newspaper editorial). With a partner, discuss which kind of writing seems better at helping the reader with unified paragraphs.

Problem probe

With a partner, use the Blueprint above to identify the problems in the following paragraphs. Do the paragraphs have unity?

1 Movie production companies should not be allowed to keep people out of public places. Taxpayers should enjoy the benefits of what they pay for with their taxes. When movies are being filmed on public roads, traffic should not be blocked. In addition, people should be able to have access to parks even when movies are being filmed. Just because some people are famous doesn't mean everyone wants their autograph.

2 Keep in mind that we live on this planet. We should care about the health of Mother Earth. Every gas is dangerous to our health. I think it is important to ratify any agreement on pollution.

3 The main difference between the public and the private health sectors is that one is free and the other is not. It means that rich people are willing to pay for health care. If there weren't a private system, the people who are using it would have to wait in the hospitals, which means more patients in the emergency room.

If feedback from your instructor or classmates tells you to focus on TOPIC SENTENCE, use this section to check the following:

Can you identify the topic?
Can you identify the focus of the paragraph (controlling idea)?

IDENTIFY THE TOPIC AND THE FOCUS (CONTROLLING IDEA)

A good paragraph needs a **topic sentence**. A topic sentence tells the reader what the paragraph is about. In the topic sentence, you must indicate what idea you will develop or define in the paragraph. Preferably the topic sentence should be the first sentence. Here are some effective examples:

» Many sources of distraction other than cell phones can affect a driver's attention.

» Some parents live their dreams through their children.

» Many factors can trigger migraine headaches.

How do you know that a topic sentence is effective? Someone who knows nothing about your topic could learn what the paragraph is about just by reading the topic sentence, without reading the rest of the paragraph.

The following are examples of unacceptable topic sentences:

⊗ My answer to this is no. (We don't know the topic.)

⊗ I think it is important for me to sleep. (Limited to personal experience.)

⊗ First, let's talk about security. (There is a topic but no focus for the paragraph.)

See what makes the following example an effective topic sentence:

Many sources of distraction other than cell phones can affect a driver's attention.

This sentence contains:

- A clear topic (the subject). The reader learns what the paragraph will examine.

  Many sources of distraction other than cell phones ...

- A focus (controlling idea). This is an idea that can be developed and supported in the paragraph.

  ... can affect a driver's attention.

MORE HELP? 👓 See Support, p. 76.

Even in a paragraph where you answer an exam or essay question, you must write as if the reader does not know the question.

BLUEPRINT FOR TOPIC SENTENCE

Check if your topic sentence matches the Blueprint.

BLUEPRINT	YOUR FINISHED PRODUCT	
Use facts that do not relate strictly to your personal experience (the use of *I* or *I think* is rare). The idea can be developed or defined.	A **topic** that is easy to identify.	A **focus (controlling idea)** that will clarify the focus of your paragraph. Make sure there is a verb.

Practice

Which of the following sentences are acceptable topic sentences for beginning a paragraph in academic, technical or professional writing? Can a reader who knows nothing about the topic know what the paragraph is about?

Determine whether there is a topic and a focus *by trying to underline* the topic and *circling* the controlling idea in each sentence.

1 Offering food is commonly used by animals during courtship.

2 I would say that I disagree with that.

3 According to a few studies on television viewing, men are in charge of the remote control more often than women are.

4 Free agency is destroying competition in sports.

5 My first argument is about the economy.

6 Another one I would like to talk about is small-market teams.

7 I think that the second one needs more help.

8 The author's use of the first-person point of view created suspense.

9 The first novel was better.

10 The setting of *Dune* is so otherworldly, yet so realistic, that the reader wants to believe it exists.

11 I think it is a good way but it is too technical.

12 Finally, let's look at the budget.

Workshop

Choose three of the ideas in the left-hand column. Use the Blueprint to expand the ideas into possible topic sentences. Check with a partner to see if your sentences help the reader learn what the paragraph is about.

IDEAS	A **topic** that is easy to identify.	A **focus (controlling idea)** that will clarify the focus of your paragraph. Make sure there is a verb.
Example • Elderly males	*Elderly males, especially over the age of 65,*	*suffer from isolation.*
• Good sales reps		
• Volunteers to test new pharmaceutical products		
• Clean drinking water		
• Effect of music		
• Individual responsibility		

If feedback from your instructor or classmates tells you to focus on SUPPORT, use this section to check the following:

> **Do you offer enough relevant examples (facts, concrete details, studies) to support your important ideas, generalizations, and opinions?**
> **Can every element of support in a paragraph be connected to the topic and focus of the paragraph?**

OFFER CREDIBLE SUPPORT

In technical and professional writing, enough relevant support must be used to confirm or illustrate each main idea. Support helps you show that what you are saying is true.

Strong and relevant support makes use of accepted facts and references such as scientific, historical or statistical data, or it uses examples to give credibility to the topic sentence of a paragraph. (See Topic Sentence, p. 73 and Relevance, p. 40.) The supporting ideas must be connected to the topic sentence. They must also stay within the boundaries of what the focus (or controlling idea) covers or defines.

Look at the possible support for the following topic sentence:

TOPIC	FOCUS (CONTROLLING IDEA)
People who are found to carry genes for certain diseases	are justified in not giving insurance companies their test results.

Possible support:

⊗ I read this and I think it is right. (Not within the limits defined by the topic sentence; can be said for just about anything you may read)

≫ A 2001 study at New York University showed that just because someone carries the gene does not mean that they will definitely get the disease. (Support: scientific study)

≫ People can willingly drink to excess or damage their health through bad eating or taking part in extreme sports, yet they are not forced to tell their insurance companies. (Support: argument)

⊗ I would not let myself be tested if I knew it meant I could not get medical insurance. (Personal opinion, not an argument)

⊗ Even if it might help me hold down my premiums, why should I trust such recent tests? (Not within the limits defined by the topic sentence; this response is personal rather than analytical)

Good support will help you do one or more of the following:

- Define, explain, clarify or illustrate an idea.
  You may classify the idea, present a solution to a problem, or develop the idea with examples to help the reader.

- Compare one idea with other ideas.
  You may look at how an idea fits in with others or how good the idea is in comparison to others (don't forget to back your idea up with facts).

- Show some effect(s) or look at cause(s).

- Give arguments (based on facts or literary passages) to demonstrate why your focus or attitude (controlling idea) is true.

HOW MUCH SUPPORT IS ENOUGH?

Many readers expect two or three relevant elements of support in each paragraph. Using sufficient details and examples will often produce paragraphs of more than 75 words. Try, however, to stay below 200 words as long paragraphs might not appear reader friendly.

Model Support 1

The following paragraph is from a text about the difficulty of measuring happiness.

> [Researchers who study why happy people are usually healthier than unhappy people are confronted with the problem of making people happy while they are sitting in a lab.] [To illustrate this, imagine that you are a researcher and you want to see the effects of anger on people.] [This is easy to do. Keep them in the waiting room of your research lab for two hours, be rude to them, and tell them horrible stories that will make them want to react negatively.] [But, in contrast, when it comes to making a person happy to be in a lab, where can researchers start?] [Do they give volunteers drugs that cause euphoria?] [If so, the researchers might end up measuring the effects of the drug rather than the person's happiness.]

Topic: researchers' problem
Focus: difficulty of making people happy in lab.

Support: illustration.

Support: clarification + cause and effect.

Support: comparison.

Support: explanation, possible solution.

Support: argument against possible solution. This confirms why the controlling idea is true: it is difficult to make people happy in a lab.

BLUEPRINT FOR SUPPORT IN PARAGRAPHS

Check if your support helps develop the topic sentence. For each element of support, use the box below to see if you can identify the kind of support you have included. As a rule, write as if readers generally expect two or three elements of support.

BLUEPRINT	YOUR FINISHED PRODUCT
TOPIC SENTENCE AND FOCUS (controlling idea)	
SUPPORT 1	
SUPPORT 2	
SUPPORT 3 (if needed)	

Support for the topic sentence should use facts to
- define, explain, clarify, illustrate
- compare
- show effects of, look at cause(s)
- give more arguments.

MORE HELP? See Transitions (p. 85) to find out which words can help you show logical relationships between ideas. See also Referencing (p. 81) if you need to quote.

See how this paragraph offers explanations and clarifications that give credibility to the topic.

The next stage of sleep, REM (Rapid Eye Movement) takes up about 20-25 percent of a normal night's sleep. REM sleep got its name because if a subject's eyes are observed, they exhibit quick movements. This stage of sleep is a very active period in which breathing becomes irregular, the heart rate accelerates, and brain wave activity increases. Sleep specialists note that this is the time when vivid dreams occur: if you wake a person up during that time, around 80 percent of the people will recall what they were dreaming. While the brain works more, REM sleep is characterized by fewer body movements than non-REM sleep. In fact, most sleepers lie virtually motionless during REM sleep.

Now look at how well the paragraph fits in the Blueprint.

BLUEPRINT FOR SUPPORT: EXAMPLE

TOPIC SENTENCE:	The next stage of sleep, REM (Rapid Eye Movement) takes up about 20-25 percent of a normal night's sleep.
SUPPORT 1	REM sleep got its name because if a subject's eyes are observed, they exhibit quick movements.
SUPPORT 2	This stage of sleep is a very active period in which breathing becomes irregular, the heart rate accelerates, and brain wave activity increases.
SUPPORT 3	Sleep specialists note that this is the time when vivid dreams occur: if you wake a person up during that time, around 80 percent of the people will recall what they were dreaming.
SUPPORT 4	While the brain works more, REM sleep is characterized by fewer body movements than non-REM sleep. In fact, most sleepers lie virtually motionless during REM sleep.

1 Support for the topic sentence of this paragraph uses facts to define, explain, clarify, and illustrate.

2 It also compares REM to non-REM sleep.

Look at the following topic sentences and possible supporting ideas. Use the Blueprint to:

• choose the idea(s) that can offer good support for the topic sentence

• identify the idea(s) that is off-topic.

1 Topic Sentence: When you get to a national park and are asked to pay, you wonder about what "public" means.

Possible supporting ideas:

a The parks really belong to the public as the maintenance is already paid by people's taxes.

b Parks encourage people to take part in healthy activities and this serves in the public interest.

c The policy only supports superficial differences between cultures, not real differences.

2 Topic sentence: In John Steinbeck's novel *Of Mice and Men*, Lennie's mental retardation makes him dependent on George.

Possible supporting ideas:

a It is true that Lennie depends entirely on George.

b George needs to protect Lennie from characters like Curly who do not understand mental disability.

c Lennie dreams of taking care of the rabbits that will be on George's dream farm.

Problem probe

MORE HELP? See Relevance, p. 40 and Disconnected Comment, p. 47.

With a partner, discuss the problems in the paragraphs below. Use the following list to identify the problems.

a No support (or not enough).

b Poorly chosen example.

c Based on prejudice or strictly personal view.

d Based on a source that lacks credibility.

e Based on insufficient data (anecdotal).

1 The government should make sure that surgeons and scientists earn more than athletes. Otherwise, it is ridiculous. Think of a man who works and the other one who catches a ball for millions of dollars. It does not make sense. This is why I think athletes should earn less.

2 The music-learning program will cost more than $90,000 to the government so it will have to be a long-term project. We should invest no more than $50,000 for research and advertising in this project because a similar project was funded last year. That project failed because they overspent in these areas.

3 Secondly, to find new workers more easily, we should offer a break that is thirty minutes long. It would be a good idea because fifteen minutes is not a lot.

4 Every local health center should open a division to teach good eating habits to anorexics and bulimics. My parents always said that good eating habits were essential. A service like this could help a lot of people to have better health.

5 In *Of Mice and Men*, there is a goal, owning land, but this goal has different meanings. For George, land is a dream come true because it gives him a place he could call his own. He wants the certainty of being happy at home. Being active on his farm is what he wants the most. An example of this is how he takes different identities to get low-paying jobs to make money.

Referencing

If feedback from your instructor or classmates tells you to focus on REFERENCING, use this section to check the following:

Did you quote properly?
Have you cited your sources properly?

A reference uses words written or spoken by someone else. References generally have one of two functions:

- In reports, they help you offer outside support for your ideas.

- In academic essays, they support your thesis and help you demonstrate that you understood what you read, for instance, in literature, the author's argument or theme.

QUOTE PROPERLY

When you use what other people have said or written to build your support, you must give proper credit to the source. Why? You do not want to be accused of stealing someone else's words, or plagiarizing. In addition, you do not want to have legal problems.

First, choose between a direct and an indirect quotation.

DIRECT QUOTATION

A **direct quotation** means using the exact words the person used in the text, presentation or interview.

A short quotation of a complete sentence integrated into your own text looks like this:

> The report stated clearly, "Every department agrees with the proposed schedule and will work to meet its deadlines."

> In *Crazy Man's Creek*, Jack Boudreau wrote, "Before radios came on the scene, people often spent months in the wilderness living in complete silence; something that is virtually unknown in today's world."

Longer passages should be indented in a separate paragraph, without quotation marks. Use a colon to introduce the quotation.

> In *To Kill a Mockingbird* by Harper Lee, Atticus made his feelings known to the children:

> > What Mr. Radley did was his own business. If he wanted to come out, he would. If he wanted to stay inside his own house, he had the right to stay inside free from the attentions of inquisitive children, which was a mild term for the likes of us. (p. 53)

INDIRECT QUOTATION

An **indirect quotation** means that you are paraphrasing an idea. In such cases, you are using someone else's idea and integrating the idea into your text.

> The report stated clearly that every department agreed with the proposed schedule and would work to meet its deadlines.

> Stanley Coren says in his book, *The Intelligence of Dogs*, that the most intelligent breed of dog is the Border Collie and the least intelligent breed is the Afghan Hound.

Practice

Turn the following sentences into indirect quotations.[1]

1 In a short letter, he admitted, "I can no longer act in the best interests of the company."

2 In *Stoney Creek Woman* by Bridget Moran, Mary John said, "1934 was a year I will never forget. The year started with both my mother and me expecting children."

3 Ms. Stewart told the staff, "I realize that the president earns as much as 150 of you. I understand your frustration that under his guidance we have been losing money every year, but he still has the power to fire every one of you."

4 Karine said, "I don't feel I need to write a conclusion."

5 The teacher confirmed to Karine, "You will repeat this course."

---

1. For help with changes to verb tenses, pronouns, and time references in indirect quotations, see *The Essentials of English: A Writer's Handbook*, by Ann Hogue, Pearson Education, 2003.

APA AND MLA MODELS
FOR REFERENCING

Here are two common ways of using references to give credit to your sources.

AMERICAN PSYCHOLOGICAL ASSOCIATION

The model for quotations proposed by the APA, the *American Psychological Association*, is commonly used in the social and behavioral sciences.

APA IN TEXT

- All direct and indirect quotations in a paper should be followed by last name of author, year of publication in parentheses. The page number will be used for direct quotes only.

  Example: (Smith, 2003)

- Direct quotations that are not introduced by the author's name include page number in addition to author and year:

  Example: In fact, we agree that: "The arts, while creating order and meaning from the seeming chaos of daily existence, also nourish our craving for the mystical." (Wilson, 1998, p. 232)

- Indirect quotations look like this:

  Example: The view held by Wolfram (2002) is that the genetic subprograms are quite simple.

- If the author is not known, use the complete title if it is short, or a few words if it is long. The title should be in italics.

  Example: (*Travels*, 2003)

APA REFERENCES

All the sources you quoted in the text according to the above model must now be listed at the end of your paper under the centered title:

References

Book:

Author's last name, first initial, year published (year in parentheses). Title of book in italics. Location of publisher: Publisher's name. Capitalize only the first word in a title and subtitle (and any proper nouns).

> Wilson, E.O. (1998). *Consilience: The unity of knowledge*. New York: Alfred A. Knopf.
>
> Wolfram, S. (2002). *A new kind of science*. Champaign, IL: Wolfram Media.

Internet Article:

Author's last name, first initial, date published or posted (the date in parentheses), title of article, name of publication or Internet site, volume number, article number. The date you found it on the Internet, the full Internet address without a period at the end.

> Swift, A. (2002, June 28). Smoking rates continuing to drop. *Health Canada Online, 2002*, Article 52. Retrieved July 16, 2002, from http://www.hc-sc.gc.ca/english/media/releases/2002/2002-52.htm

Articles:

Articles from magazines, newspapers, and journals follow the same pattern.

Author's last name, first initial, date of publication, day, month, or season (date material in parentheses), title of article, name of publication (*in italics*), volume number (*in italics*), page numbers.

Magazines:

Armstrong, L. (2002, Summer). How to be happy. *Geist Magazine, 45,* 40-46.

Hornby, N. (2002, July 15). We are the world. *The New Yorker,* 32-36.

Newspaper:

Bronskill, J. (2002, August 10). Woman fired over guide dog. *The Vancouver Sun,* p. A3.

MODERN LANGUAGES ASSOCIATION

MLA stands for the *Modern Languages Association.* Its guidelines are often referred to as *MLA style.* It is commonly used in the humanities.

MLA IN TEXT

- All direct and indirect quotations in a paper should be followed by (Last name of author, page). Put in parentheses, without the abbreviation p. for page:

  Example: (Smith, 118)

- If you already mention the author's name in the sentence, just put the page number in parentheses (173).

- Direct quotations that are not introduced by the author's name include the page number in addition to the author (separated by commas).

  Example: In fact we agree that: "The arts, while creating order and meaning from the seeming chaos of daily existence, also nourish our craving for the mystical." (Wilson, 232)

- Indirect quotations look like this:

  Example: The view held by Wolfram is that the genetic subprograms are quite simple (384).

- If the author is not known, use the complete title if it is short, or a few words if it is long. The title should be in quotation marks followed by the page number.

  Example: ("Travels," 42)

MLA REFERENCES

All the sources you quoted in the text according to the above model must now be listed at the end of your paper under the centered title:

Works Cited

Book:

Author's last name, first name, the title of the book in italics or underlined, with capital letters for all important words, location of publisher (with state or province if city isn't familiar): name of publisher, date of publication.

Wilson, Edward. O. *Consilience: The Unity of Knowledge,* New York: Alfred A. Knopf, 1998.

Wolfram, Stephen. *A New Kind of Science,* Champaign, IL: Wolfram Media, 2002.

Internet Article:

Author's last name, first name, title of article (title in quotations), name of publication or site, date of electronic publication, latest update or posting. If numbered, pages, paragraphs or sections. If mentioned, name of institution sponsoring the website.

Date you found the article <full internet address> in angle brackets.

Swift, Andrew. "Smoking Rates Continuing to Drop." <u>Health Canada Online.</u> 28 June 2002. 16 July 2002 <u><http://www.hc-sc.gc.ca/english/media/releases/2002/2002-52.htm></u>.

Articles:

Author's last name, first name, title of article in quotations, title of publication in italics or underlined, date of publication, page number.

Magazines:

Armstrong, Luanne. "How to Be Happy." <u>Geist Magazine</u>, Summer 2002: 40-46.

Hornby, N. "We Are the World." *The New Yorker,* 15 July 2002: 32-36.

Newspaper:

Bronskill, Jim. "Woman Fired over Guide Dog." *The Vancouver Sun,* 10 Aug. 2002, A3.

Transitions

If feedback from your instructor or classmates tells you to focus on TRANSITIONS, use this section to check the following:

Should you add transitions to help your reader see how your ideas are connected?

To make a text easier to read and understand, you must connect its various parts to achieve **cohesion** and **coherence**. A text has cohesion when the logical organization of its writing is easy to see. Using *and, but, then* and *so* works well in speaking, but academic and professional writing gains effectiveness with more sophisticated connectors.

WHAT DO CONNECTORS CONNECT?

Some connectors link two **clauses**. A clause is a group of words that contain a subject and a verb, e.g., *Martin was certain.* When a clause, such as *Martin was certain*, can have full meaning even when used alone, it is called an **independent clause**. An independent clause can form a **simple sentence**.

Some clauses have no complete meaning when used alone, for example, "*because the new manager had told him.*" A clause like this is called **dependent** or **subordinate** because it must be attached to another clause called the **main clause**: *Martin was certain because the new manager had told him.* The word *because* connects the two clauses to form a complex sentence.

MORE HELP? See Varied Sentence Types, p. 142.

USE A HELPFUL TRANSITION

The following chart compares different types of connectors.

Subordination or Transition Signal?

	ONE SENTENCE		ONE OR TWO SENTENCES
	These connectors link ideas within one sentence.		These connectors can link ideas within one sentence (with a semi-colon;) or between two sentences.
	COORDINATION	SUBORDINATION	TRANSITION
COMMON FUNCTION OF THE CONNECTOR	**Coordinating conjunctions** connect two independent clauses together. They are usually placed at the beginning of the second independent clause.	**Subordinating conjunctions** are placed at the beginning of a subordinate (dependent) clause to introduce that clause.	Transitions such as the **conjunctive adverbs** below show a relationship between two independent clauses or between two sentences. They can be placed in different positions in the clause, e.g., before or after the subject. See the chart on p. 88.
ADDING AN IDEA	And	Who(m), that	Also, besides, furthermore, in addition, moreover
CONTRASTING	But, yet	Although, even though, whereas, while	However, nevertheless, on the other hand, still
GIVING A CHOICE / SETTING A CONDITION OR A LIMITATION	Or (nor)	If, unless	Instead, otherwise
SHOWING CAUSE AND EFFECT	So	As, because, since, so that	As a result, therefore, consequently, thus, hence

Here are some correct uses of connectors:

a Coordination between two independent clauses

> *Examples:* We will survey the students, and we will post the results on our website.
>
> We surveyed the students, but they don't agree with the motion.

b Subordination between main clause and subordinate clause (or subordinate and main)

> *Examples:* The evening show is sold out although many seats are available for the matinee.
>
> Since temperatures were lower than normal, the snow accumulation was higher.

c Transition from sentence to sentence

> *Examples:* Some scientists are not good at public speaking. Nevertheless, they may have a lot of important things to say.
>
> I was hoping that they would choose our advertising campaign. Instead, they chose the other one.

Choosing the right transition makes a text clear and coherent by helping the reader follow your thinking. The wrong transition can lead to confusion.

⊗ Our idea is easy to develop. We will make profits in the first year. (Not effective because the reader has to figure out the connection between these two sentences.)

⟫ Our idea is easy to develop. As a result, we will make profits in the first year.

Sometimes the transition you choose is inappropriate because it does not show the relation you have in mind.

⊗ We want our project to be funded; nevertheless, we are the most qualified team.

⟫ We want our project to be funded because we are the most qualified team.

TRANSITIONS BETWEEN CLAUSES OR SENTENCES

Transitions, such as the conjunctive adverbs in the following chart (p. 88), guide the reader. They should make the order of your ideas and the shades of meaning in your text easy to understand. They can connect ideas found in two independent clauses, or they can link an idea from one sentence to the next sentence.

> Cora Deschamps felt bad in the city. Konrad DeVille, **however**, liked the night life.

Note: Many grammar guides recommend the use of a semi-colon (;) when a conjunctive adverb is at the beginning of the second independent clause:

> Cora Deschamps felt bad in the city; Konrad DeVille, however, liked the night life.

COMMONLY USED TRANSITION SIGNALS

FIRST IDEA	TRANSITION SIGNALS	SENTENCE 2 (OR INDEPENDENT CLAUSE 2)
In the boxes below, the first idea can be an **independent clause** or it can be a **sentence**. Conjunctive adverbs are not used to connect single words, phrases or subordinate clauses.	The **conjunctive adverb** can be at the beginning of the second sentence. It can often be between the verb and the subject: *Mary, however, agreed.*	With a conjunctive adverb, the second idea **cannot** be just one word, a phrase or a subordinate clause. You need a sentence.

SHOWING TIME OR SEQUENCE

FIRST ACTION, EVENT OR SITUATION	TIME OR SEQUENCE SIGNALS	ACTION, EVENT OR SITUATION THAT FOLLOWS OR COVERS A TIME PERIOD
Ms. Fox came up with a very successful promotion for the CD.	Afterward, At the time, Next, Soon, Then,	… Mr. Raven wanted more.
	Meanwhile,	… the artist signed with another company.
Hard work used to be the formula for success.	Nowadays	… hard work and networking are needed.

SHOWING CAUSE AND EFFECT (OR RESULT)

CAUSE	CAUSE AND EFFECT SIGNALS	RESULT
One of your colleagues stole money from the cash register on several occasions.	As a result, Consequently, Therefore,	… the store installed cameras to check on employees.
	Thus, (more formal)	… we must take new security measures.
	Hence, (very formal)	… we no longer retained his services.

ADDING AN IDEA

FIRST ACTION, EVENT OR SITUATION	ADDITION SIGNALS	IDEA, ACTION OR EVENT YOU ARE ADDING
Brian Dade took his boss's car without permission.	Also, Besides, (*often used to add a negative idea, or a category that is a bit different*) Furthermore, In addition, Moreover,	… he was seen stealing a newspaper.

COMPARING OR SHOWING SIMILARITY

FIRST IDEA BEING COMPARED	SIMILARITY SIGNALS	IDEA THAT IS LIKE THE FIRST ONE
Moe Sheen-Saul spent three months in jail after the road rage incident.	Likewise, Similarly,	… his friend Bib Bavette was found guilty.

CONTRASTING IDEAS

FIRST IDEA	CONTRAST SIGNALS	IDEA THAT SHOWS A DIFFERENCE WITH THE FIRST IDEA
Konrad DeVille was never found guilty.	However, Nevertheless, Still, Yet,	… many questions remain unanswered.
A leader must show strength.	On the other hand,	… a leader must have compassion.
Ms. Segal wanted a transfer to Sydney, Australia.	Instead,	… she was sent to Sydney, Nova Scotia.

SETTING A CONDITION OR ADDING A LIMITATION

FIRST IDEA	CONDITION OR LIMITATION SIGNAL	IDEA THAT WOULD NOT HAPPEN WITHOUT THE CONDITION OR LIMITATION
Often people have to learn new skills on the job.	Otherwise,	… they will not be able to perform their jobs effectively.

PART 123

TRANSITIONS

COMMONLY USED TRANSITION SIGNALS

ADDING EMPHASIS TO SHOW THE IMPORTANCE OF AN IDEA		
FIRST IDEA	EMPHASIS SIGNALS	IDEA THAT SHOWS THE IMPORTANCE OF THE FIRST IDEA
Do we know enough about photosynthesis?	In fact, Indeed, Obviously,	… it is important to ask if we could find out more.

Practice

Part A. Check the meaning of the connectors in the list above. Then, in the second sentence of each pair of sentences below, use the connector that will help you show a meaningful transition.

Example: (*however / similarly*) Violence in schools is widespread. This doesn't make it any more acceptable.

> *Violence in schools is widespread. This, however, doesn't make it any more acceptable.*

1 (*therefore / yet*) The rescuers are all volunteers. Due to helicopter costs, rescue missions are expensive. _____

2 (*indeed / yet*) All teachers believe that their students can learn. Too many teachers are still prejudiced against students whose learning styles differ from their own.

_____

_____

3 (*otherwise / therefore*) Her test was positive. The doctor prescribed some medication.

_____

4 (*indeed / next*) Fears of mass cloning should not worry us. Most scientists recognize the need for diversity. _____

_____

5 (*thus / otherwise*) You must file your income tax return on time. You will incur penalties if you owe the government money. _____

_____

Part B. Choose three of the following independent clauses. Refer to the charts (p. 86, pp. 88-90) to add an appropriate coordinating conjunction or conjunctive adverb and a second independent clause. Discuss your new compound sentences with a partner.

Examples: Car alarms are not necessary. *Many people, however, feel safer knowing their car is secure.*

Restoring a work of art requires a lot of time. *Furthermore, there is often a long period before funding can be obtained.*

1 It is not necessary to buy designer clothing. _____

_____

2 The media have some negative effects. _____

_____

3 The natural environment needs to be protected. _____

_____

4 Many companies have already created electric cars. _____

_____

5 Having accidentally set fire to the couch, he rushed next door in his pajamas. _____

_____

TRANSITIONS BETWEEN PARAGRAPHS

Many writers use transition signals to show a sequence of ideas such as a series of arguments, steps in a process, or time in chronological events. These signal words are usually found in the topic sentences of paragraphs.

- *First / To begin with,*

- *Second / This is followed by*

- *Third,*

- *Finally / This brings us to the final argument ...*

MORE HELP? 👓 See Topic Sentence, p. 73.

Conclusion signal words:

- *To conclude / In conclusion / To sum up / In short / For these and other reasons*

Usage | Hint:
Note that *First of all* is used in speaking but is not often found in writing.

Conclusion

If feedback from your instructor or classmates tells you to focus on CONCLUSION, use this section to check the following:

> **Is there a conclusion?**
> **In the conclusion, have you confirmed your thinking?**
> **Have you made clear what the reader should remember?**
> **Have you restricted or expanded your ideas?**

END WITH A CONCLUSION

Don't make the reader reach the end of your text and ask "Is this all there is?" Make sure your text has a conclusion. Otherwise it may give the impression that you ran out of ideas and just stopped writing.

An appropriate conclusion in research reports and papers will

- confirm your thinking

- point to what the reader should remember

- limit or expand on what you wrote.

Although not all of the elements listed below are present in the conclusion of every essay or piece of literary analysis, you may retain the parts that will help you offer a sense of closure to your text.

CONFIRM YOUR THINKING

Ask yourself:

- Why are you right in saying what you say in your conclusion?

- Can people understand the logic you used in guiding them to what you want them to remember?

If it helps to make your main point clear, restate in simpler terms any main point, essential information, or even your thesis. (**Note:** Some readers consider restatement less effective.)

Examples of confirmed thinking:

1 In conclusion, newspapers have tight deadlines that do not allow the writer to check all the facts, while book writing is a long-term process that leaves room for careful research....

Restatement

2 [As the evolution of the chicken industry in the United States shows,] factors such as selective breeding, economic problems, scientific developments, and new technologies can work together to change the way the population perceives its sources of food....]

Main point

POINT OUT WHAT THE READER SHOULD REMEMBER

What would you want your readers to remember in three weeks about what you wrote?

State the main point you want people to remember.

- What generalizations can you draw? (Which of the facts or ideas you considered can work for a larger group of people or situation?)

- What do you regard as really important in what you wrote?

Examples:

1 In conclusion, newspapers have tight deadlines that do not allow the writer to check all the facts, while book writing is a long-term process that leaves room for careful research. As such, newspapers should not be primary sources of information in academic research.

2 ... Pets should be allowed to visit their owners in the hospital because the benefits to patients outweigh the risks.

LIMIT OR EXPAND

Show the limitations of your work and state any questions that remain.

Ask yourself these questions:

- Where do we go from here?

- What will follow?

LIMITATIONS

LIMIT

Every report or essay has limited scope. You cannot cover everything. In what you do cover, what limitations or uncertainties might there be in your analysis? What conditions are necessary?

Before we can estimate whether changing to a new system would really save us money, more research on the cost of staff training needs to be done.

QUESTIONS THAT REMAIN

EXPAND

Is there any future action that you anticipate or wish for? In a letter or a report, it can refer to what you expect as the result of the letter or report. In an essay, you can express a broader vision for opening new future perspectives that might apply specifically to your text. In research reports, you can make suggestions about future research that is needed.

Usage Hint:

In many countries that used to be under British influence, people use the British "our" spelling in such words as *behaviour* and *honour,* instead of the American "or" spelling (*behavior* and *honor*). In these countries, other words may also be spelled differently. For example, people may use the British "re" spelling for such words as *centre* and *theatre,* instead of the American "er" spelling (*center* and *theater*).

Our research, however, suggests that it is important to explore the use of pets as therapeutic agents working with individual patients in institutional settings ... Selected patients might be given their own pets or have a pet visit them on a regular basis. Further research using behavioural measures and experimental strategies appropriate for single cases is needed to examine the effect of such programs. [1]

Your suggestions must not be too general; they must apply specifically to your text. Do not give the feeling that your conclusion could apply to all texts.

⊗ Let's hope that in the year 2020, things will be better.

⊗ I hope that researchers will find a solution.

Problem probe

Discuss with a partner how you would improve the following conclusions. Ask these questions:

- Has the thinking been confirmed?

- What is the reader expected to remember?

- What will follow?

- Do we learn about the limitations or the questions that remain?

- Is the conclusion too general? (For example, could the conclusion be used at the end of many other texts and still work? If so, it is too general.)

- Is the conclusion too specific to be able to offer a sense of closure?

1 In conclusion, we saw that many strategies can be used. I hope that the population will be more careful about this.

2 To conclude, it is true that we have to do something.

3 I hope that with the above measures, in the future the problem will be solved. I hope that these measures help you.

4 I hope you will consider my point of view on all aspects of this project. It would be good for you to support our project.

5 In conclusion, I support decreasing the number of smokers.

1. Fairnie, H and Winkler, A. (1988) The importance of pets for institutional elderly. In D. Boldy and C. Rhys-Hearn (Eds.) *Systed 87 – Systems Science in Health-Social Services for the Elderly and the Disabled.* The International Institute for Systems Science in Health Care: Perth.

Apply the conclusions you write to the Blueprint below. See if you have included elements that are useful in giving the reader a sense of closure. Indicate which part of the conclusion corresponds to the part in the left-hand column.

BLUEPRINT	YOUR FINISHED PRODUCT
Confirm your thinking.	In conclusion, To sum up, As we saw,
Make clear what the reader should remember (e.g., in a letter, any action that you wish for).	
Limit or expand. (Be specific enough to apply to your text / not so general that it applies to any text)	

Problem probe

Use the criteria in the Blueprint to decide which of the conclusions below are effective and which need to be improved. Discuss with a partner and present your view.

1 Clearly, freedom of speech is at risk when the ownership of the media is too concentrated. Stricter laws are necessary to ensure that no one person can own too many newspapers.

2 The sense of direction has not atrophied altogether in modern people. Most of us are vaguely aware of this sense, if only by comparison with other people who tend to get lost more easily or who are much better at finding their way. Nevertheless, in the absence of artificial aids, most modern people are poor navigators compared with nonhuman animals. This is no doubt why we find the abilities of dogs and cats so fascinating, and why homing pigeons are especially intriguing. They can do something we can't. They have sensitivities that we have lost.[2]

3 The health care system is one of the major problems in our society. We are all aware of this but what can we really do about it?

2. Sheldrake, Rupert. (2000) *Dogs That Know When Their Owners Are Coming Home*, New York: Three Rivers Press, p. 192.

4 In conclusion, the health system has many problems. We know from experience that if only one aspect of a problem is eradicated, we will create something else to worry about.

5 As we saw, although the meaning of land ownership may differ for Duddy Kravitz and Scarlett O'Hara, the importance they attach to it makes both characters act in a way that destroys personal relationships. Can today's people empathize with the protagonists of Mordecai Richler's and Margaret Mitchell's novels? Carefree college students who might choose friends over property will not. But perhaps we should consult couples going through divorce proceedings to ask for a second opinion.

6 People will continue to make illegal photocopies of copyrighted material because it is easy to do, there is little risk of getting caught, and they don't want to pay money to buy the rights. The publishing industry will have to make it easy to click and pay or it will suffer financial ruin.

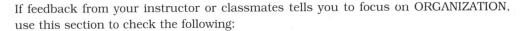

Organization

If feedback from your instructor or classmates tells you to focus on ORGANIZATION, use this section to check the following:

> **Is the organization of your writing correct in relation to task and purpose?**
> **Does your organization make the reader's job easier?**

Usually, a reader can see structure in a text by recognizing the development of ideas in paragraphs and by following the sequence of ideas with transition signals. However, work-related and academic writing often include within the text predictable **patterns of organization** that guide the reader through complex ideas.

Several types of organization can help you refine the presentation of your ideas within a text. This section examines the following types of organization: definition, comparison, process, cause and effect.

CHECK APPROPRIATENESS TO TASK AND PURPOSE

Writing in your professional life is rarely for entertainment. You have a **purpose**: a problem has to be examined or solved, or a situation must be explained. See which of the patterns below can help you organize information clearly and coherently.

DEFINITIONS

Whether you work in advanced technology, business, research, government or industry, words must be accurate so that people can agree on what they mean. This makes definitions useful in serious writing.

Why would you define terms? Even when people use the same terms, they attach different meanings to them. For the same reason, dictionaries are sometimes of limited help: they might give you many different definitions for the same word, or the definitions might be incomplete for your purpose. In addition, sometimes you need to define a term that is made up of more than one word.

A good definition usually contains a classification: placing a term in relation to a group or category.

Examples:

A phobia means an intense fear.

Infertility refers to the inability to conceive a baby naturally .

Once you have classified the terms in a category, you can add distinguishing characteristics such as appearance, function, restrictions. For instance, what makes the term different from other terms in the same category?

A phobia means an intense fear associated with a specific event or situation even if there is very little danger.

The characteristics you include in a definition can allow you to focus on expressing a meaning that matches your task and purpose. For instance, the characteristics might help answer a specific need: *When would you start treatment for infertility?* If you use the definition of the World Health Organization, this is the answer:

Infertility refers to the inability to conceive a baby naturally after trying for two years .

Consider, however, all the emotional and financial implications the characteristics of a definition can contain. In North America, when the medical profession needs to decide when to begin treatment, the following definition is preferred:

Infertility refers to the inability to conceive a baby naturally after trying for one year.

This means that many couples begin worrying a year earlier and start spending on treatment a year earlier.

WHEN DO YOU NEED TO USE A DEFINITION?

Generally, when people have to set rules, achieve a common basis for discussion or pose a problem, they need to define terms. Here are some cases where you should include a definition.

- **You think any of your readers or any members of your audience do not know what the term means.**

    Examples:

    Photobiology is the branch of biological science that studies the interactions of light with living organisms.[1]

    "Clinical trial" is the scientific term for a test or study of a drug or medical device in people. These tests are done to see if the drug or device is safe and effective for people to use.[2]

---

1. *Photobiology Online.* 13 April 1999. http://www.kumc.edu/POL/ASP_Home/what_is.html
2. "Why Volunteer? Clinical Trials of Medical Treatments," 7 Dec. 2002. http://www.fda.gov/opacom/lowlit/cltr.html

- **There are many possible meanings or interpretations for the term.**

    For example, when Health Canada looks at the word "drug," its definition excludes "recreational" drugs bought on the street:

    > Drugs include both prescription and nonprescription pharmaceuticals; biologically-derived products such as vaccines, serums, and blood derived products; tissues and organs; disinfectants; and radiopharmaceuticals.[3]

- **You want to compare two terms to see how they are the same and how they are different.**

    Example:

    > Although many people confuse the two terms, social scientists treat prejudice and discrimination as distinct phenomena. **Prejudice** is a negative, hostile social attitude toward members of another group. All members of the group are assumed to have undesirable qualities because of their group membership. **Discrimination** refers to actions carried out against another person or group because of his or her group membership. In particular, it is the denial of opportunities that people would grant to equally qualified members of their own group.[4]

- **You want to use a term in a special way in a presentation, report or official document.**

    Some organizations need to define terms in a very specific way. Such a definition might affect a lot of people or involve a lot of money. For example, see what happens when people try to agree on what the term "vegetable" means:

    > Officials of the European Union are meeting behind closed doors today to rule whether a lumpy sauce is, legally speaking, a vegetable …

    > At present, a sauce containing more than 20 percent in lumps is classified as a vegetable, even if the lumps are fruit, triggering import taxes that can reach 288 percent.[5]

    As you can see, a vegetable can be a fruit sauce.

    Some definitions will clearly state what something is not. For example, at the end of its definition of *documentary*, Telefilm Canada specifically excludes some categories from funding:

    > Projects presenting information primarily for its entertainment value are not considered to be documentaries. These include such ineligible genres and programming formats as life-style "how-to" (e.g., gardening shows, cooking shows, home decorating shows, etc.) programming.[6]

3. "How Drugs are Reviewed in Canada," *Health Canada* Magazine. 16 April 2002.
   http://www.hc-sc.gc.ca/hpb-dgps/therapeut/zfiles/english/fact-sht/fact_drug_e.html

4. Tepperman, L. and Rosenberg, M. (1995) *Macro/Micro: A Brief Introduction to Sociology*. 2nd Edition. Scarborough: Prentice Hall. p. 179.

5. "EU logic: Lumps Turn Sauce into Vegetables," *National Post*, 10 Jan. 2002. p. A1.

6. "Guidelines." *Canadian Television Fund 2002-2003*. 28 Sept. 2002.
   http://www.televisionfund.ca/pages/guidelines/documentary/pdf

With a partner, check the following definitions.

Part A. Correct the problems.

1 The definition omits some elements needed to answer the task or pose the problem.

⊗ Science is everything that surrounds us. Every little part of nature is science.

_____

_____

2 The definition does not take current knowledge into account. (See Task 2, p. 102.)

⊗ A mother is the woman who gives birth.

_____

_____

3 The definition is circular.

⊗ A scientist is a person who works in a field related to science.

_____

_____

4 The definition can apply to another term.

⊗ A mother is a person who gives genetic traits, like blue eyes. It's the person who gives you half your DNA.

_____

_____

Part B. Identify the problems.

1 Technology is everything that has to do with electronics.

2 Advertising is when you want people to know about a product or a service so you advertise. You can find advertising on TV, and in magazines or newspapers.

3 A mother is a woman who has made the decision to take care of children.

4 A network is something that connects computers together.

PART 12**3**
ORGANIZATION

Check if the definition you gave matches the Blueprint.

BLUEPRINT	YOUR FINISHED PRODUCT
THE TERM	
THE CLASS OR CATEGORY in which the term can be placed.	
THE CHARACTERISTICS that allow the reader to understand what makes this term different from any other term and (*if necessary*) the characteristics that help with your task or purpose.	

Practice

Among the terms *food additive, microwaves, regulation* and *standard*, circle the ones that are defined in the paragraphs below. For each term defined, underline the major elements of the definitions you found (term, class/category, characteristics).

1 Is there a Difference Between a Standard and a Regulation?

In the lexicon of the Scope and Standards Committee, standards of practice means the expectations of peers in the application of optometric knowledge, skill and judgment when providing care to patients. Using this definition, standards of practice will improve the likelihood of effective patient outcomes. It is acknowledged, however, that there is room to exercise professional judgment depending on the specific clinical situation. If challenged, a practitioner would have to convince his or her peers that the standard had been applied and how this was achieved. If this was before a tribunal, such as the Discipline Committee, the testimony of expert witnesses might be used to determine what ought, or ought not, to have been done.

A regulation relating to practice provides little discretion to the practitioner. For instance, the Records Regulation requires optometrists to record specific information. Failure to comply with the regulation could result in a finding of professional misconduct. Before a tribunal, the mere demonstration of non-compliance with the regulation without the testimony of an expert witness may be sufficient.[7]

2 Microwaves are used to detect speeding cars, to send telephone and television communications, and to treat muscle soreness. Industry uses microwaves to dry and cure plywood, to cure rubber and resins, to raise bread and doughnuts, and to cook potato chips. But the most common consumer use of microwave energy is in microwave ovens. That use has soared in the past decade.

What is Microwave Radiation?

Microwaves are a form of "electromagnetic" radiation; that is, they are waves of electrical and magnetic energy moving together through space. Electromagnetic radiation ranges from the energetic x-rays to the less energetic radio frequency waves used in broadcasting. Microwaves fall into the radio frequency band of electromagnetic radiation. Microwaves should **not** be confused with x-rays, which are more powerful.[8]

3 A food additive is an ingredient that is added to foods to aid in processing, preservation, or quality improvement. Additives should not be used to disguise faulty or inferior manufacturing processes or to conceal damage or spoilage; only the minimum amount of an additive necessary to achieve desired results should be used.[9]

Workshop

Individually, define one of the terms below using the Blueprint for help. Then compare your definition with a partner's to see if your definitions can be improved.

Task 1: Is professional wrestling a *sport*?

The Canadian Broadcast Standards Council, the national body that self-regulates the broadcasting industry, received viewers' complaints about the "sick and obscene" nature of a *Monday Night Raw* broadcast ... As well, the Council received a complaint about the "vulgar, sexist and violent" nature of a *Raw is War* broadcast. Both programs were on TSN, The Sports Network.[10]

7. Bulletin, The Official Publication of the C.O.O (College of Optometrists of Ontario), June 2000. 2 Feb. 2002. http://www.collegeoptom.on.ca/bulletins/june2000.asp

8. "Microwave Oven Radiation." U.S. Food and Drug Administration: CRDH (Center for Devices and Radiological Health) Consumer Information. 21 July 2002. http://www.fda.gov/cdrh/consumer/microwave.html#2

9. Hurst, William C et al. "Getting Started in the Food Business." University of Georgia College of Agricultural and Environmental Sciences. http://www.ces.uga.edu/pubcd/b1051-w.html

10. Owens, Anne Marie. (2001, April 11) "Broadcast Regulator Rules on Complaints against WWF Shows." *National Post*, p. A3.

TSN did not provide viewer advisories coming out of every commercial break to warn about the violent nature of the program as there is some expectation of violence upon watching sports on television. Before the Council can rule on the viewers' complaints, it needs to decide whether professional wrestling as shown in World Wrestling Entertainment broadcasts is indeed a sport. Offer your help by defining *sport*.

Task 2: Who is a *mother*?

The Law Reform Committee has asked you to give a clear definition of the word *mother* so that it becomes clear whose name can appear as a mother on a birth certificate. The information below provides the context.

Surrogacy Case Ends in Court Battle Over Names on Birth Certificate

A month after they were born, a baby boy and his twin sister still have no birth certificates. The paperwork is being held up in a dispute that could change the legal definition of "mother" in Massachusetts.

In Massachusetts and many other U.S. states, only the woman who gives birth is presumed to be the mother and can have her name on the original birth certificate. The law does not address instances in which women become mothers by having their embryos implanted in a surrogate.

Marla and Steven Culliton hope to change that.

They hired a surrogate after Marla had six miscarriages. The woman was implanted with an embryo created from the couple's sperm and egg, and on July 23 she gave birth to the Cullitons' twins.

The surrogate, known in court as "Melissa," has no biological link to the children, and she agrees she has no parental rights.

Still, a family court judge refused to allow the Cullitons' names on the original birth certificates.

"It is one of a new wave of cases which are forcing courts throughout the country to wrestle with the meaning of such basic, fundamental terms as 'mother,' 'paternity' and 'maternity' as a result of technological advances in reproductive medicine," said Melissa Brisman, the Cullitons' lawyer.

"What we're asking this court is, 'What does it mean to be a mother?' and 'Does the mere act of giving birth give rise to motherhood?'"[11]

Task 3: Define poverty as it applies to Americans. Can your definition remain the same if you apply it to an African country?

Task 4: Define *science* and *technology* so that we can distinguish between them.

---

11. Lavoie, Denise, with files from Tom Arnold, (2001, Aug. 30). *National Post*, p. A10. Reprinted with permission of *The Associated Press*.

PART 1 2 3
COHERENCE

COMPARISON

Similarities and differences can be found in practically everything. Pointing out obvious ones or putting two things together side-by-side does not mean that you are making a serious comparison. For instance, how useful is the following?

⊗ One is blue, the other one is red. One is cheap, the other one is expensive.

Your job as a writer is to help the thinking of your readers. Organizing a comparison is not limited to putting ideas side-by-side.

Some writers use analogy, which is a form of comparison, to explain ideas or concepts that are unfamiliar. See p. 54 for more on analogy.

WHAT IS THE PURPOSE OF YOUR COMPARISON?

In academic and professional writing, a comparison is done for a purpose, for example, showing relationships between ideas, evaluating a product, or reviewing the performance of employees. (See Purpose, p. 62.) Your comparison must be developed to guide the reader in seeing which thing is better or which idea makes more sense. A good comparison makes it clear what you intend to show at the end, so as you write, always keep your purpose in mind.

Practice

Good comparisons are done for a purpose. Can you match the purposes in the left-hand column with the comparisons in the right-hand column?

PURPOSE OF THE COMPARISON (REASON FOR WRITING)	WHAT ARE YOU COMPARING?
__4__ To show relationships between ideas or theories (also including academic critique).	1. Successful vs. unsuccessful crime-prevention strategies.
_____ To evaluate a product.	2. Organic vs. non-organic food labels.
_____ To conduct a review (for example, of personnel).	3. Two employees to see who is better.
_____ To establish labeling regulations.	4. The themes used in two pieces of literature.
_____ To help train employees.	5. The new computer system with the old one.
_____ To distinguish a pattern (for example, in police work).	6. Two cars to see which one is better.

WHAT IS BEING COMPARED?

Before you start, you must be clear on what you want to compare, for instance:

When does advertising become propaganda?

Workshop

Read the first two paragraphs to identify the subject of the comparison in each.

Point 1: Functions of man talk: _____

Point 2: Functions of woman talk: _____

Do Women Talk More?

Research suggests that more talk is associated with higher social status or power … Evidence collected by American, British and New Zealand researchers shows that men dominate the talking time in committee meetings, staff meetings, seminars and task-oriented decision-making groups. If you are skeptical, use a stopwatch to time the amount of time contributed by women and men at political and community meetings you attend. This explanation proposes that men talk more than women in public formal contexts because they perceive participating and verbally contributing in such contexts as an activity which enhances their status, and men seem to be more concerned with asserting status and power than women are.

By contrast, in more private contexts, talk usually serves interpersonal functions. The purpose of informal or intimate talk is not so much status enhancement as establishing and maintaining social contact with others, making social connections, developing and reinforcing friendships and intimate relationships. Interestingly, the few studies which have investigated informal talk have found that there are fewer differences in the amount contributed by women and men in these contexts. Women, it seems, are willing to talk more in relaxed social contexts, especially where the talk functions to develop and maintain social relationships.

Now examine paragraph 3. The subject is "kind of talk." What are the points being

compared? _____

Another piece of evidence that supports this interpretation is the kind of talk women and men contribute in mixed-sex discussions. Researchers analyzing the functions of different utterances have found that men tend to contribute more information and opinions, while women contribute more agreeing, supportive talk, more of the kind of talk that encourages others to contribute. So men's talk tends to be more referential or informative, while women's talk is more supportive and facilitative.[12]

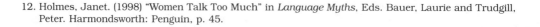

12. Holmes, Janet. (1998) "Women Talk Too Much" in *Language Myths*, Eds. Bauer, Laurie and Trudgill, Peter. Harmondsworth: Penguin, p. 45.

Good comparisons are usually built around criteria that can be examined for both items or ideas that are being compared. Choose a comparison you need to develop and put together the ideas you can use.

THE SITUATION

Give background and purpose (the reason for your comparison).

•

Define the problem.

•

POTENTIAL BENEFITS OR STRONG ARGUMENTS FOR	POTENTIAL RISKS AND DISADVANTAGES OR COUNTER-ARGUMENTS (ARGUMENTS AGAINST)
• •	• •

By choosing points that can be organized according to similarities and differences, you will show the reader which of the subjects (people, things or ideas) seem preferable for your purpose.

A COMPARISON DON'T

Don't limit your comparisons to a pair of separate descriptions. This might leave the reader with the task of doing the comparison.

CAN YOU SHOW HOW TWO POINTS OF COMPARISON ARE RELATED?

To make sure that the ideas you use are fully integrated in the comparison, use transitions that allow you to build references from one point of comparison to another. See the list in the Blueprints on pp. 106-107.

There are two simple ways to organize a clearly structured comparison.

COMPARISON BLUEPRINT 1:
POINT-BY-POINT (or alternating pattern)

With this pattern, you choose a point of comparison and examine it in relation to both items or ideas. Try to have an equal number of elements of comparison for each thing you are comparing.

Check if your comparison matches the Blueprint. Indicate which parts correspond to the parts in the left-hand column (e.g., 1A / 1B).

BLUEPRINT	YOUR FINISHED PRODUCT	HELPFUL TRANSITIONS
Point 1 for A Point 1 for B		Although As opposed to But By contrast However
Point 2 for A Point 2 for B		Likewise On the contrary On the other hand Similarly Still
Point 3 for A Point 3 for B		Unlike Whereas While Yet

In a point-by-point comparison, you take every point you wish to compare and see how it compares to another. For instance, if someone needs advice in choosing between contact lenses and glasses, you can look at three points and compare each point as it relates to both contact lenses and glasses.

Point 1: Durability
    A. *Of glasses*
    B. *Of contact lenses*

Point 2: Physical restrictions and comfort
    A. *Of glasses*
    B. *Of contact lenses*

Point 3: Cost
    A. *Of glasses*
    B. *Of contact lenses*

COMPARISON BLUEPRINT 2:
SUBJECT-BY-SUBJECT (or block-by-block pattern)

With this pattern, take the first item being compared and look at all the details (e.g., characteristics, opinions) for it. Then you look at **parallel details** about the second item.

Check if your comparison matches the Blueprint. Indicate which parts correspond to the part in the left-hand column (e.g., A1 / B1).

BLUEPRINT	YOUR FINISHED PRODUCT	HELPFUL TRANSITIONS
Subject A Point 1, 2, 3		Although As opposed to But By contrast However Likewise On the contrary On the other hand
Subject B Point 1, 2, 3		Similarly Still Unlike Whereas While Yet

Using the same example as above, the comparison would be organized as follows:

Subject A: Glasses
     1. *Durability*
     2. *Physical restrictions and comfort*
     3. *Cost*

Subject B: Contact lenses
     1. *Durability*
     2. *Physical restrictions and comfort*
     3. *Cost*

Subject-by-subject development may also mean that in the first paragraph, you study all the differences while in the second paragraph you study all the similarities.

Which of the two models should you choose? Consider your task and purpose, outline your ideas with Getting Started on a Comparison, p. 105, and choose which organization seems more natural in the context.

Use the Blueprints (pp. 106-107) to determine whether the paragraphs below are arranged point-by-point or subject-by-subject.

1 **Purpose: Getting Ready for College**

High school teachers and college professors are trained differently and have different expectations. Students need to be aware of the characteristics of each in order to be successful in college. One difference is that high school teachers usually check completed homework assignments whereas college professors may not check homework at all, yet professors will assume that students can do the same tasks on a test. In terms of office hours, high school teachers are frequently available to talk with students before, during and after class while college professors expect students to see them during scheduled office hours. Another difference is that high school teachers are trained in teaching methods and often write notes on the board for students to copy. College professors, on the other hand, are trained in their specific subject area and expect you to take notes as they lecture. Finally, high school teachers will often approach students if they think the students need help and remind the class of approaching deadlines. College professors are usually open and friendly, but expect students to contact them if they need help.

2 **Purpose: Identifying Bad Sleepers**

Sleep specialists are often overwhelmed with the number of people who think they have a sleep disorder. Yet the differences between a good sleeper and a bad sleeper are generally easy to identify: a good sleeper generally falls asleep in less than ten minutes after going to bed. Another characteristic is that the good sleeper does not usually wake up during the night. Researchers note that good sleepers remain virtually motionless.

Whereas about three quarters of the population should be considered good sleepers, about 25 percent are bad sleepers. Bad sleepers often take an hour or more before falling asleep. Contrary to good sleepers, they awaken one or more times during the night. They also tend to move a lot, and many of them sleep on their back. In addition, many people with psychological disorders can be labelled as bad sleepers.

Problem probe

Can you see how the passages below fail to integrate a purposeful comparison? With a partner, discuss what should be added to ensure that these comparisons become useful.

1 I was asked to choose one of the projects. I did not like the first project so I will discuss the second one.

2 Even though Toronto had "Victory" gardens in both wars, Toronto has not been a hotbed of community gardening and it has been difficult to get the issue on the political agenda. Toronto barely caught the last wave of enthusiasm for community gardening in North America in the early 1970s and still lacks a cohesive, comprehensive community gardening consciousness.

There are twenty-six community gardens in eleven municipalities in the Greater Vancouver Regional District (GVRD). The city of Vancouver has the most, a dozen community gardens, nine of these in parks or park reserves with 580 community garden plots. The city of Burnaby has the next highest number of gardens, three, but the number of available allotments is equal to the city of Vancouver. The rest of the gardens are spread amongst nine other municipalities. Greater Vancouver has a total of about 2000 plots. Most community gardens have a waiting list, despite not advertising.[13]

Workshop

Write a point-by-point or subject-by-subject comparison that examines one of the questions in the list below.

Before you begin your comparison, you must determine your purpose. Here are some possible purposes (you can also use your own):

- show relationships between ideas or theories
- establish principles
- evaluate a product
- distinguish a pattern
- conduct a review

See Practice, p. 108, for more ideas. Then determine the points that you wish to compare from the list below.

1 Private or public health care: Which is better?

2 Living in a big city: What are the advantages and disadvantages?

3 Animal and human communication: Do animals have language?

4 Private or public schools: Are the differences real or perceived?

5 Traditional selective breeding of domestic animals or genetically engineered improvements: Is one more acceptable than the other?

6 Multiculturalism: Does it work or does it build walls?

7 Female or male boss: Is one style better than the other?

8 Spending money more wisely: Who can do a better job, you or your government?

9 Government grants: Do they help our society or do they encourage inactivity?

10 Consumers: Do we really need the latest version of new technologies?

Usage Hint:

Transition signals useful in comparisons:

Although
As opposed to
But
By contrast
However
Likewise
On the contrary
On the other hand
Similarly
Still
Unlike
Whereas
While
Yet

---

13. Cosgrove, Sean. "Community Gardening in Major Canadian Cities: Toronto, Montreal and Vancouver Compared." *City Farmer, Canada's Office of Urban Agriculture.* 13 July 2002
http://www.cityfarmer.org/canadaCC.html

PART 1 2 3
ORGANIZATION

PROCESS

A process is a sequence of steps done in order. In work-related or academic writing, a process can be used to guide people who have to perform a task or to explain how something works.

To write out a useful process, you must build an unbreakable chain. Each step needs the other steps in order for the process to work. In addition, the steps must be relatively equal in what they tell the reader to do.

THE STEPS IN A PROCESS MUST LOOK AS SIMILAR AS THE LINKS IN A CHAIN.
DON'T MAKE YOUR PROCESS LOOK LIKE THE CHAINS ABOVE.

Model Process
How to Ensure that New Drugs Are Safe

Have you ever wondered how a drug prescribed by your doctor was approved by the government as safe? In the United States, a new drug goes on sale only after many years of careful studies. As part of the process that gets prescription drugs to the market, companies that develop pharmaceutical products are expected to study the following.

Testing the drug on human cells and proteins

First, during a stage called discovery, potential new drugs are tested in the laboratory to see what effects they have on human cells and proteins. This step may show some potential benefit of the drug or may indicate that the drug is toxic.

Testing on animal species

During the stage called pre-clinical research, the drugs are tested as humanely as possible on various species of animals to simulate the complexity of the human body. This step allows scientists to see how the drug is absorbed and eliminated. It also helps to measure the effectiveness of the drug as well as its toxicity and side effects in conditions similar to human illnesses.

Studying the effect on healthy human volunteers

Next, if the drug is proven safe in animals and the drug is believed to have the potential of becoming effective in the treatment of some disease, the pharmaceutical company must obtain permission from the government (the Food and Drug Administration) to do clinical trials on humans, also called clinical research studies. This is referred to as Phase I trial: about twenty to one hundred human volunteers are given the new drug in various doses. Phase I lasts about one year and tries to see if the drug is safe on humans. About 75 percent of the drugs tested will make it to the next step.

Studying the efficacy of the drug

If Phase I shows that the drug is safe, researchers move to Phase II studies: efficacy. The researchers recruit hundreds of patients that have the medical condition or disease that the drug is expected to treat. Over a period of several years, the effects of the drug on the health of patients is examined. This is done by comparing a group of patients getting the new drug and a group of patients getting a placebo (a sugar pill). If the new drug is found to be sufficiently effective and safe, the study goes to Phase III.

Confirming the effectiveness and safety

When the drug goes to Phase III studies, the drug treatment is given to thousands of patients with the specific disease or condition under study. Over a period that can take up to five years, researchers look for results that confirm the drug's effectiveness. They also monitor side effects and collect additional information about safety. For example, they check what happens if the drug is used in combination with other drugs available on the market. The drug is also compared to commonly used treatments to see if it is more effective. After this stage, if the drug is both safe and effective, and if the benefits are proven to outweigh the risks, the drug will be approved for sale by prescription to the general public.

Monitoring the general population

Finally, even after the drug has been approved for sale through a prescription by the FDA, studies continue. Under Phase IV, the manufacturer monitors problems in the general population to report any rare side effects, rectify doses, or even to recommend new uses of the drug that were not initially anticipated.

As you can see, the process of getting a drug from discovery to the drug store is long, usually between ten and fifteen years, and demanding. Generally, of 5,000 to 10,000 potential new drugs examined under the initial discovery stage, about 250 make it to the next stage—animal trials. Only five drugs will usually show enough potential to go on to clinical trials in humans. Of these five, only one will be approved for sale. So, can you all feel a little safer now?

CHECK	YOUR TEXT	LANGUAGE FOCUS
WHOM ARE YOU WRITING YOUR PROCESS FOR? Make sure that the reader knows whom you are writing for. Must your description be general enough to be understood by anyone? Should your description be just for experts?		**Are your transitions between steps clear?** Use transitional words: *next, later, afterward, after that, first, second, when, because, as a result, following that, just before …*
WHAT IS THE PROBLEM? Will readers know right from the start what problem you intend to solve?		**Have you made the steps parallel?** Begin steps with words that have equal grammatical value (e.g., start with gerunds *-ing* or start with verbs in the imperative).
WHAT IS THE PURPOSE OF YOUR DESCRIPTION? • Do you want to explain something? • Do you want people to make a decision based on your description? • Do you want people to act in a specific way?		**Have you used action verbs?** Some verbs are common in describing processes: *choose, select, open, attach, take (is / are taken to), request, place, put, insert, load, turn, add, remove, get, send (is sent), move, close, test.*
WHAT MAJOR STEPS DO YOU NEED TO INCLUDE IN YOUR PROCESS? Have you included all essential information? If you try to apply the process, does it work?	• • • • •	**Have you used verbs appropriately?** (See p. 129) The *imperative mood* is helpful if you want to tell how to do something. The *present tense* is common in scientific explanations of processes.
IS THERE ENOUGH SUPPORT? Readers don't like to be told what to do. Add reasons for following your steps. If you just say "Don't smoke," you will have less effect than if you explain briefly why.		The *past tense* is common in reports of processes used in experiments by other researchers.
CAN YOUR READER UNDERSTAND EACH OF YOUR STEPS? Is it always clear who does what, or what affects what? Ask a friend to read your process to see if it is clear or if any step is missing.		The *passive voice (am, is, are, was, were + past participle)* is common when the focus is on the action to be performed rather than on the person doing it.

Workshop

DESCRIBING A PROCESS

Choose one of the topics below and apply the Blueprint to write a process.

Practice by following these requirements:

- Your process must include at least six steps.

- Write at least two sentences for each step.

- Use transitions like *when, because, as a result, following that, then, for instance, for example.*

- Use action verbs.

Task 1: Choose a process you are familiar with and describe it. It may be related to your field of study. For example, you could explain how something works or must be installed. You may also choose to write about a task you perform at work.

Task 2: Research one of the following to develop a process.

1 How to measure intelligence.

2 How to get clean water.

3 How to tell a fake from an original (e.g. a piece of art; a bootleg product).

4 How the price of gas is set.

5 How to tell a good poem from a bad one.

6 How to pay less for what we buy (legally, of course).

7 How computers can recognize people.

8 How to ensure security in the use of credit cards.

9 How to control violence.

10 How to control biker gangs.

11 How to protect the population against a virus.

12 How to make math courses exciting.

13 How a business can protect itself against employee fraud.

14 How to promote a product.

15 How to decide if a food is "healthy."

Task 3: You have just become the editor in the newsroom of a newspaper. Your job is to decide which articles and news items will be published out of the thousands that you receive every day. On your nights off, the assistant editors make the decisions. To ensure consistency in publication, you want to be sure that the articles your assistants choose are the same as the ones you would select. Explain your criteria in a six-step process that will help your assistants make the same decisions you would make.

Task 4: Use the information in *Persuasion: The Process of Changing Attitudes*, p. 114, to develop a process that will help someone write more persuasively. The skills you describe will be helpful in marketing or even in an academic essay.

> **Usage Hint:**
> To know if your process is good, ask someone to apply it. If the person follows the process and gets the results you wanted, the process is successful.

The effort to change attitudes—or at least to try to change them—seems to grow ever more intense. Television commercials, magazine ads, giant billboards, political campaigns, public service announcements, and even documentary films are all used to urge people to do something—for example, to vote one way or another, to stop smoking, or to start exercising. The messages and the media vary, but the goal remains the same: to change people's beliefs and ultimately, their behaviour. (...)

To what extent are attempts at interpersonal **persuasion** effective? And what determines whether persuasion will succeed?

In most cases, attempts at persuasion involve a source directing a message to a target audience. Early research on persuasion, therefore, focused on those basic components and addressed various aspects of this question: "Who says what to whom and with what effect?" The findings of such research were complex, but among the most important were these:

1 Experts are more persuasive than non-experts. We give more weight to arguments delivered by those who seem to know what they are talking about.

2 Messages that appear not to be designed to change our attitudes are often more successful than ones that seem intended to manipulate us. We do not trust information that we believe was meant to be persuasive.

3 Popular and attractive sources are more effective in changing attitudes than unpopular or unattractive ones. Personal appeal is important, particularly in politics, as many of our politicians have found out.

4 Individuals who are relatively low in self-esteem are often easier to persuade than those who are high in self-esteem. These people are more susceptible to persuasion from high-status or attractive sources.

5 When an audience holds attitudes contrary to those of a would-be persuader, it is often more effective to adopt a two-sided approach, in which both sides of an issue are presented. When members of an audience hold attitudes consistent with those of a would-be persuader, however, a one-sided approach is often more effective.

6 People who speak rapidly are generally more persuasive than ones who speak slowly, partly because they seem more competent and confident and expert.[14]

In addition to using information from the text above, you can also consider that other studies have shown that people often perceive rhyming statements as more accurate than similar statements that don't rhyme. For example, the line "haste makes waste" is seen as more accurate than "haste makes inefficiency."[15]

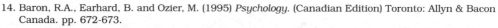

14. Baron, R.A., Earhard, B. and Ozier, M. (1995) *Psychology.* (Canadian Edition) Toronto: Allyn & Bacon Canada. pp. 672-673.

15. From a study at Lafayette College published in *Psychological Science.* Reported in *National Post,* 7 Nov. 2000, p. C9.

Discuss the problems in the following processes based on Task 3 in the Workshop, p. 113.

Example:

PROCESS: NEWS SELECTION	COMMENTS
Analyzing the world issues.	What questions do we need in the analysis?
Analyzing the impact.	The impact on whom?
Finding the audience.	Shouldn't this be pre-established? So why would this be a step in the decision-making process? Should have been decided at another level.
Biggest audience.	Grammar: not parallel, confuses the reader. Besides, this point is not necessary if you understand the above.
Similar issues.	Grammar: not parallel. What does this mean?
I would choose the most interesting stories because my first step is to interest the readers.	"Choosing" is the goal, not a part of the process. What is the first step?

Now, offer your own comments on this process.

PROCESS: NEWS SELECTION	COMMENTS
Classify the articles according to the writer's level of education.	
Classify the articles by the accuracy of the subject: give each a mark.	
Classify the articles according to originality.	
Would it be easy for my type of reader?	
It also depends on the precision and length of the article.	
Add the marks you gave each article and publish the articles with the best marks.	

CAUSE AND EFFECT

Many of the texts that are written in academic or professional life contain segments in which the writer examines a cause and its effect or results.

In connecting cause and effect, you must consider details and facts that are relevant to the context. For instance, to answer "What makes the alarm clock go off?" you have to figure out which of the numerous causes can apply to the context, to the task or to the purpose.

- In a technical discussion, the reader would expect explanations of the mechanisms involved in making an alarm clock go off.

- In a technical manual, the user would expect to be told what buttons to use to make the alarm clock go off.

- If the context is an unhappy person waking up, the cause might be "I saw our son playing with the alarm clock yesterday," or "I forgot that it was Saturday and I did not turn the alarm off last night."

Choose a cause and effect relationship that is relevant to the context or to your task and purpose.

Model Cause and Effect
Factors Promoting Self-Sacrifice

In the following passage, Eric Hoffer examines why some people might be willing to die for an idea. The context is an analysis of the phenomenon.

Effect

To ripen a person for self-sacrifice, he must be stripped of his individual identity and distinctness. He must cease to be George, Hans, Ivan or Tadeo—a human atom with an existence bounded by birth and death. The most drastic way to achieve this end is by the complete assimilation of the individual into a collective body. The fully assimilated individual does not see himself and others as human beings. When asked who he is, his automatic response is that he is a German, a Russian, a Japanese, a Christian, a Moslem, a member of a certain tribe or family. He has no purpose, worth and destiny apart from his collective body; and as long as that body lives he cannot really die.[16]

Cause

---

16. Hoffer, Eric. (1951) *The True Believer*. New York: Harper & Row. (Perennial Ed. 1966) p. 60.

There are many types of organizations possible in cause and effect papers. Make sure that for every cause, there is one or more corresponding effects, results, or consequences.

There can also be more than one cause for an effect or result.

In a paragraph you can check:

CAUSE(S) YOU HAVE IDENTIFIED	TRANSITION(S) (IF USEFUL)	CORRESPONDING EFFECT(S) FOR EACH CAUSE

You may also discuss the effects first and then work toward the causes.

EFFECT(S) YOU HAVE NOTED	TRANSITION(S) (IF USEFUL)	CORRESPONDING CAUSE(S)

Example:

EFFECT(S) YOU HAVE NOTED	TRANSITION(S) (IF USEFUL)	CORRESPONDING CAUSE(S)
Student fails course	because	• missed classes. • did not do some of the assignments.

If your text is covering a chain reaction, you can organize it as follows:

GENERAL: CAUSE 1	EFFECT 1 WHICH IS ALSO CAUSE 2	EFFECT 2 WHICH IS ALSO CAUSE 3	EFFECT 3 (CONSEQUENCES, RESULTS OF THE PROBLEM / ISSUE YOU ARE DISCUSSING)

Practice

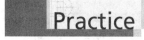

Analyze the following paragraph to see the cause and effect relationships.

The effect of light is such that people exposed to light signals that lack periodicity cannot remain in sync with the world around them. Disturbed sleep, reduced alertness, hunger at irregular times are among the predictable consequences affecting shift workers, jet travellers, or even students who keep erratic sleep schedules based on forthcoming exams. Whenever our body clocks have to be reset, we all experience jetlag. In fact, some researchers contend that the phenomenon informally known as "Monday morning blahs" is caused by the body's attempt to reset its clocks after the altered weekend schedule. Studies show that people who keep the same routine for bedtime and for waking up during the weekend are apparently less affected by Monday mornings. The rest of the people more or less jetlag themselves into tiredness.

Now fill in the blanks in the chart on the next page to show you understand the cause and effect relationships.

CAUSE	EFFECT / CONSEQUENCE / RESULT
	Disturbed sleep, reduced alertness, hunger at irregular times.
Body clocks need to be reset.	
	Monday morning "blahs".
Keeping the same routine during the weekend.	
Not keeping the same routine during the weekend.	

Workshop

Invent a purpose to answer one of the questions below. Then, write one or two 75-word paragraphs in which you examine cause and effect relationships that may explain the following.

1 What causes road rage?

2 Why do students drop out?

3 Why do people cheat on taxes?

4 Why is it difficult for people to find jobs after they complete college?

5 How does divorce affect children?

6 How do computers improve quality of life?

7 Why are there more women in higher education?

8 Does constant listening to the same version of a song or musical piece make us think that this version is the only true interpretation?

Identify as many cause and effect relationships as you can in the paragraphs below on the evolution of the chicken industry.

1 Today's genetic engineering and the constant attempt to improve the characteristics of animals had an ancestor: selective breeding, that is, choosing only the animals with valuable characteristics for reproduction. One of the first events that was going to change the North American outlook on chickens was that in the 1830s some farmers began selective breeding of chickens as a hobby, allowing only the best chickens to reproduce. The result of that was the development of better breeds of chickens, birds whose genes were reliable. Before the 20th century, a hen would, on average, lay thirty eggs a year. By the 1930s, a good hen would lay about a hundred eggs a year. Today's hens produce over 250 eggs a year.

2 As people realized in the 1920s that they could make money by raising chickens, they began buying them by the hundreds. This meant that chickens could no longer be fed leftovers. Chicken feed was needed. That's when food science became a factor. The science of chicken nutrition contributed to the development of superior food. Among the changes was the introduction of vitamin D that helped take care of rickets, a disease that makes the bones soft. How spectacular were the changes? In the 1930s, it took just over 6 pounds of feed to produce 1 pound of chicken meat; in 1943, it took between 4 and 5 pounds; today just over 1 pound is needed. Such an improved ratio of food/weight-gain also meant a fall in the price of chickens as feeding became less expensive.

PART 3

LANGUAGE USE AND EXPRESSION

Clarity
Reader Friendliness

A good writer makes the reader's job easier. A reader who must constantly make an effort to understand what you are writing might be tempted to stop trying to understand and reject your ideas.

In academic and work-related writing, your texts must be **clear and reader friendly**.

Clarity means that you are not making your reader guess what you are trying to say.

Reader Friendliness means that you bear your readers in mind and use a style that most readers will consider appropriate.

Part 3 explains how to make your writing clear and reader friendly.

If feedback from your instructor or classmates tells you to focus on CLARITY, use this section to check the following (See also Reader Friendliness, p. 135):

> **Did you check the meaning of key terms?**
> **Did you choose terminology appropriate for the context?**
> **Did you include vocabulary that can add precision to your text?**
> **Did you check if grammar mistakes affect your meaning?**
> **Did you check if sentence structure changes the meaning?**

Clarity in a text means that the reader does not have to stop and ask, "What is this supposed to mean?"

As a guiding criterion, ask yourself or ask a classmate: **Can the reader easily understand everything without having to read again?** To achieve clarity, avoid sentences like these:

⊗ There are differences between multiethnic languages, but not between multi-racial languages.

⊗ We evaluated each subject accidentally to see what advantages each one offered.

⊗ It would be expensive for the government to irradiate poverty.

⊗ "What I think, I don't like to think. So, when I don't like to think about things, I think about things I like to think about. If you start thinking about it, you get really concerned."[1]

CHECK THE MEANING OF KEY TERMS

If a reader tells you that something is unclear, checking your terminology is a good place to start improving. Writing clearly means that key terms (the words that are absolutely necessary for your topic) should be used correctly. Sometimes even simple terms are incorrectly used.

In work-related and academic writing, numbers are often key terms. Make sure they add up and that their presentation is clear.

Problem probe

With a partner, discuss the problems with key terms in the sentences below.

1 Electricity in apartment buildings would no longer be needed since it would be replaced by energy.

2 I hope you realize that the government should act on what I propose in the near present.

3 When the market went down, he sold all the actions he had in General Electric.

---

1. Baseball manager Tony La Russa, commenting on a strike by baseball players. *National Post*, 22 Jan. 2001, p. B5.

4 The cost for the uniforms is $10,000 while salary costs will run to $110,000. Rented equipment and space will come up to $15,000. With the fees of $300 paid by the 100 participants, we expect the total project cost will be $155,000.[2]

5 I would give them the biggest half of the money.

CHOOSE TERMINOLOGY APPROPRIATE TO THE SITUATION OR CONTEXT

CONTEXT

When looking up a word in a dictionary, make sure you know in which context you want to use the word. This will allow you to choose which exact meaning applies to your text.

For instance, consider the word *chip*. A computer *chip*, a potato *chip*, and a *chip* off the old block are three different terms. Each meaning of *chip* depends on the word's context.

Context may also mean geographical differences in usage. Think of *fish and chips*. Such *chips* in England are known as French fries in the United States and Canada.

Similar differences can affect the cost if you forget that the word *dollar* used in the United States does not have the same value as a dollar in Canada. Be aware of context before you choose a term.

Workshop

With a partner, discuss the meanings of the boldfaced words in the following expressions.

1 **sound** advice; **sound** engineer; Puget **Sound**

2 dog **pound**; **pound** on the door; a **pound** of butter

3 **mean** man; **mean** number; have the **means**

4 **survey** people; **survey** a piece of land

5 **seal** on a leaking pipe; official **seal**; well-trained **seal**

AMBIGUITY

The fact that many English words can have different meanings in different contexts forces you to pay attention to ambiguity. **Ambiguity** means that something is not clear because there could be more than one meaning. Make sure your sentence does not have two or more interpretations.

---

2. For help in using numbers, see *The Essentials of English: A Writer's Handbook,* by Ann Hogue, Pearson Education, 2003.

Examples:

1 Men's Room out of order. Please use floor below.

In addition to what we walk on in a house, *floor* can mean a story in a building: "This elevator stops on the 46ᵗʰ floor." In the above example, men were asked to use the bathroom located one story below, but the sign could have another meaning.

2 Many police officers would benefit from race training.

Some readers could be surprised with the next sentence:

This would help them be more sensitive to the problems of some minorities.

Most readers would anticipate this:

This would help them be more physically fit.

It would have been better to include the idea of *race sensitivity training* in the first sentence.

COLLOCATION

You should also pay attention to **collocation**, the fact that some words are often found together. For instance, usually the word *forecast* will be used in a context where either the word *weather, economic* or *sales* is also used. For your English to sound natural in a given context, you must check to see which words are often associated. For example, native speakers generally expect a rabbit to *hop* and a frog to *leap*.

Practice

Use the following contexts to decide which word is needed. Discuss the differences with a partner.

bite / sting	hardly / hard	policy / politics
sued / prosecuted	salary / wage	pretty / handsome
searchers / researchers	fees / fare	law / bylaw

Example: A bee will _____*sting*_____ while a mosquito will _____*bite*_____.

1.1 The main character was a very _____ man.

1.2 The main character kept looking at _____ women.

2.1 The federal government passed the _____ about six months ago.

2.2 The town councilors disagreed about the new _____.

3.1 No refunds is the store _____.

3.2 He went into _____ at a very young age, being elected for the first time at 23.

4.1 The _____ were out all night looking for the lost boy and his dog.

4.2 The _____ used new parents to complete a study on sleep deprivation.

5.1 We had to pay over $1200 in legal _____ to show that our cat was not responsible for the damage.

5.2 Do you have any idea how much the bus _____ is between Reno and Las Vegas?

6.1 Our neighbor, who had a daycare center, was arrested by the police and will be _____ for misconduct.

6.2 We _____ our neighbor when one of her trees fell on our car and she refused to pay for the damage.

7.1 She tried really _____ because she wanted the job badly.

7.2 He _____ tried because he didn't care.

8.1 Many of the student jobs available pay little more than minimum _____.

8.2 I have nine years of experience as a federal civil servant, so my _____ expectations seem reasonable.

Problem probe

Use a dictionary to find the problems in collocation in the following sentences. State the correct term.

1 Many older people wear a set of unreal teeth. _____

2 The hotel has a golf court next door. _____

3 Under "Experience" in a man's job résumé: ⊗ barmaid.

4 The fertilized egg that was implanted in the surrogate mother was not her personal egg. _____

5 The document caused a lot of interest. _____

Write the answers in the right-hand column.

BLUEPRINT	
Word or term you want to check:	
• What is the context or situation (e.g., psychology, sports, Europe, …)?	
• Is any other meaning possible in another context? (Check dictionary.)	
• If yes, which meaning applies in the present context?	
• Is the term used only with certain other words (collocation)? • If so, what are the words?	

CHOOSE THE RIGHT WORD

As a writer, you should constantly try to expand your vocabulary. If most of the verbs in your texts are *be, have, go, get, take*, chances are that you need to improve your choice of words.

Few English words have exact synonyms. Many words with similar basic meanings have subtle shades of difference between them. Choosing a word with the most precise meaning for a specific context helps you develop a more effective piece of writing. For instance, many terms with specific meanings can replace a general word like *look*. Some alternative terms are *watch, stare, glance, glare, gaze, peek, ogle* and *peruse*. Consider the following thesis statement:

> In Irwin Shaw's story, "The Girls in Their Summer Dresses," Michael's ogling epitomizes the destructive lack of respect traditionally displayed by men.

How different would the thesis statement be if we changed *ogling* to *staring* or *glancing*? Use a dictionary[3] to find the differences in meaning among the terms in the diagram

---

3. Some dictionaries such as Longman's *Language Activator* and *Collins COBUILD Dictionary* are helpful in finding out slight, but important, differences in meaning.

below. For instance, while the meaning of *look* is general, the other terms have more specific meanings. Part of their specific meanings sometimes overlap, but not completely. Only perfectly synonymous words would be placed in the same oval. For instance, how is *glare* different in meaning from *stare*?

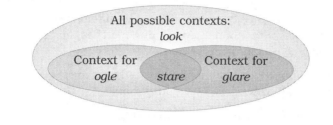

Practice

With partners, choose two of the series of words below and research the differences in meaning. Use dictionaries, the Internet, or help from your teacher to find examples that clarify how each term can best be used.

Example: Laugh: *giggle; guffaw; chuckle*

"Giggle" is to laugh nervously, for instance, at a job interview, or it can be trying to laugh quietly without being noticed (in class after everybody else has stopped laughing).

"Guffaw" is laughing very loudly, bursting into laughter like an explosion.

"Chuckle" is to laugh quietly, to yourself, sometimes with a funny clucking sound, a bit like a chicken.

1 Change: *fluctuation, turnaround, upheaval*

2 Fake: *knock off, artificial, synthetic*

3 Improve: *upgrade, streamline, fine-tune*

4 Part: *share, stage, cross-section, segment*

5 Say: *state, declare, claim, allege*

6 Information: *advertising, publicity, propaganda*

CHECK UNCLEAR GRAMMAR

Grammar is a set of rules that helps us use language so that other people can understand us. Sometimes, not using the correct grammar rule changes the meaning.

See how the plural form might suggest an incorrect interpretation in this example:

> We would like to hire the second candidate because she has had a lot of experiences with youngsters.

What about the difference between a criminal and a police officer?

> He followed a criminal path.
> She followed a criminal's path.

Common clarity problems caused by grammar are examined below.

CORRECT PRONOUN REFERENCE

Clarity can be improved if you pay attention to pronoun references. In work-related and academic writing, choose a pronoun reference that matches the point of view needed in your text and keep a consistent point of view.

- Use the first person (*I, we*) to report what you did or want to do. Remember to limit the telling of personal experiences in serious writing.

    We added an ingredient to the frog's food every week.

- Use the second person (*you*) to explain how to do something or perform a procedure.

    Remove any excess water before you continue.

Note: The use of the second person sounds a little more informal.

- Use the third person (*he, she, it, they*) to explain what others did or to show what happened.

    The subjects were asked to identify a sequence of three colors. They then had to push a button.

Now read the sentence below to see how difficult it is for the reader to understand the meaning when the pronoun reference is not clear.

⊗ The budget to launch a satellite may seem expensive, but after a few years, it will be cheaper.

What does *it* mean? Will the launching budget be lower? Will the satellite be cheaper to maintain? Will the satellite generate income that will make the launching look cheaper?

Compare:

I think it is a great piece because she is so original.
I think it is a great piece because it is so original.

Problem probe

Discuss the following problems with a partner. What makes the sentence hard to understand?

1 I will discuss the salary of professional athletes who are too big.

2 The presenters want to find the poorest school in the area and get food to these schools every morning so that they can serve breakfast to the pupils of this school.

3 We need to stop obesity before it gets bigger.

4 People who talk to their plants get better results unless they also need to be watered.

5 Some commercials should be presented to children in which they explain the dangers of gambling.

MORE HELP? For help with pronoun references, see *The Essentials of English: A Writer's Handbook,* by Ann Hogue, Pearson Education, 2003.

VERB TENSES AND TYPES OF INFORMATION

Verbs tell the reader *when, how long, a fact or condition,* and *who / what caused* the action. Follow these guidelines:

- Refer to previous writing or research with past tenses.

    In her study on eating disorders, Professor Goldwater *interviewed* 56 subjects over a period of three months.

- Define and describe with the present or past tense.

    The movie *begins* with a violent scene. OR
    The movie *began* with a violent scene.

- Analyze in the present when possible.

    The main character *blames* most of her mistakes on her lover.

- Give instructions in the present.

    Either in the imperative mood:

    Take the bottom left corner and *fold* it.

    OR in the indicative mood:

    First, you *take* the bottom left corner and you *fold* it.

- In reports, choose the passive voice if you want to focus on what happened rather than on who or what caused or performed the action. You should, however, try to use the active voice whenever possible. Compare:

    Active: We injected the rats with the experimental drug.

    Passive: The rats were injected with the experimental drug.

But pay attention to verb endings.

Compare the endings of active and passive forms:

1 We will be glad to use your products if you can show that they are improving.

We will be glad to use your products if you can show that they are improved.

2 Your point of view must be changed.

Your point of view must be changing.

Once you have decided on the present or past sequence for a description, respect the rules for that sequence.

In addition, use a grammar book to check the difference between the simple past (finished, completed past) and the present perfect. Compare the different meanings in the use of verbs:

Jacinthe worked in our department for five months. (she has finished)

Jacinthe has worked in our department for five months. (she began five months ago and continues)

Jacinthe is working in our department for five months. (and then she'll be transferred)

MORE HELP? 👓 Check the use of the progressive form (especially in letter writing; verb tense sequence in indirect quotations; and conditional forms and sequence of tenses in *The Essentials of English: A Writer's Handbook,* by Ann Hogue, Pearson Education, 2003.

CHECK PROBLEMS IN SENTENCE STRUCTURE

Sometimes the words are clear and the grammar is perfect, but the text is still unclear because of bad syntax. What is **syntax**? Syntax is the sentence structure you need to use in order to give clear information. In English, the most common pattern is:

S	V	(O)
SUBJECT (WHO OR WHAT)	VERB (ACTION OR STATE)	OBJECT OR COMPLEMENT (WHAT HAPPENS TO THE SUBJECT OR WHAT FOLLOWS THE VERB): OPTIONAL
Example: Most of our colleagues	adopted	the second method.

OMISSIONS

Did you forget a word? Check omissions because a missing word can change the meaning. Compare:

> The exploding deer offers wolves a stable food source.

> The exploding deer population offers wolves a stable food source.

Compare: Can you see which presenter is a stock broker and which one is a marketing manager?

> I am going to explain which companies we should sell.

> I am going to explain which companies we should sell to.

NEGATIVES

Don't overuse negative forms. If you use a negative form, make sure it does not contradict something else you are saying. If you find two or more negatives in the same sentence, see if any of them can be taken out.

Can you see how these sentences might make reading more difficult? Discuss with a partner.

1 If a woman is not a person who has no biological links with the baby, I think she can't be a mother because she is not the real one.

2 We shouldn't sell human organs to other humans because they need them so we don't.

3 I have always lived in my parents' house and I do not feel satisfaction because I worked hard to get this house.

PHRASES AND CLAUSES

Just like single words, English **phrases** and **subordinate clauses** can be used as subjects or objects. Be aware of this as you construct sentences.

A **phrase** is a group of words that together do not contain a subject and a verb.

Picking up empty bottles.

In this example, the phrase *Just before lunch* is the subject:

Just before lunch is a good idea.

A **subordinate clause** is a group of words that contains a subject and a verb.

What Rita said.

However, a subordinate clause has no meaning alone. Subordinate clauses must be attached to a main clause.

What Rita said was very clear.

A subordinate clause that is not attached to a main clause is a **sentence fragment**. It needs work to become a clearly expressed thought. A subordinate clause used alone is meaningless:

although the protagonist knew the truth.

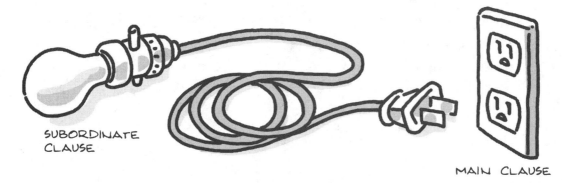

SUBORDINATE CLAUSE

MAIN CLAUSE

A SUBORDINATE CLAUSE WORKS ONLY WHEN IT IS CONNECTED.

Discuss the problems that syntax can cause by comparing the pairs of sentences below.

1.1 We need to study what rabbits can eat in this area.

1.2 We need to study what can eat rabbits in this area.

2.1 The dog that treated the veterinarian had rabies.

2.2 The dog that the veterinarian treated had rabies.

3.1 She wants to know where might be found the reference.

3.2 She wants to know where the reference might be found.

Practice

The inability to identify subjects leads to many mistakes, particularly in subject-verb agreement. Underline the subjects: nouns, pronouns, gerunds (-*ing*), phrases or clauses. Then use the correct present-tense form of the verb. Be sure that the verb agrees in number with the subject.

Example: The <u>decisions</u> that we will be making (depend) _____*depend*_____ on many factors.

1 The first three trees (have) _____ to be cut.

2 Sunscreen lotions (be) _____ not available at the camp.

3 Dogsledding, unlike bobsledding, which has some Jamaican participants, (be) _____ popular only in northern climates.

4 The books I found while I was walking to school (seem) _____ to be for a course on mnemonics.

5 Each member of both departments (be) _____ expected to submit a written report tomorrow.

6 The boss and you (have) _____ to develop a common view on the solution.

7 What the finance manager and the head researcher don't agree on (be) _____ the cost of equipment.

8 Just before sunset (be) _____ a good time to come back.

9 Contaminating the water tables (be) _____ a serious offense.

10 What she suggests in her report (be) _____ a real eye-opener.

LENGTH OF SENTENCES

Sometimes a sentence becomes less clear because it contains many ideas that are not connected clearly.

⊗ After examining the first criterion, which to me seems to be the highest priority, and I am talking about safety, I have decided that the flood protection system that was submitted to our company by Rivera Plumbing meets our standards and should be bought.

In general:

- Try to keep the verb near its subject.

- Use simple sentence structures for complex ideas.

- Don't put your most important ideas in subordinate clauses (a subordinate is an assistant; it does not have the main responsibilities).

- Don't try to put too many ideas in one sentence.

≫ We should buy the flood protection system submitted by Rivera Plumbing. It meets our standards and our first priority, safety.

Discuss the problems in the sentence below.

⊗ After we tried the first method, we saw that it took too much time and that it was also the most expensive, we decided to reject it.

Even when there are many ideas, the structure should be as simple as you can make it.

If a sentence is unclear to your reader, check for the following:

- There is a subject and a verb.
- The subject is not too far from the verb.
- If the sentence is long, make sure you know the subject and the verb for each clause.
- The most important idea is not in the subordinate clause.

SUBJECT: WHO OR WHAT	VERB: ACTION OR STATE	IF NEEDED
• noun / pronoun • gerund (*-ing*) • phrase • subordinate clause	• What happens? OR • What is the situation?	• What adds information to the subject of the action or to the verb itself?

Practice

Use the Blueprint to unpack the information below to create shorter sentences. Use transitions if useful. Do not put important ideas in subordinate clauses.

1 When you realize that the results of your water purity test did not come out right and when you know that water is used by the population, you must not take chances, because we know that there have been problems with *Escherichia coli (E. coli)* before, although the advisory might be found to have been unnecessary, the citizens must be warned immediately.

2 Because the car was tested, we discovered that despite many safe trials which were done by a non-biased team of researchers where the air bags did not blow up, occasionally they did.

3 We analyzed the report that the environmental engineer had given us and decided that it would be too expensive to go ahead with the project, and since we had other ideas already, we decided to choose one of those in the hope that it would better fit our budget, but we will definitely make our decision before next week.

Reader Friendliness

If feedback from your instructor or classmates tells you to make your text READER FRIENDLY, use this section to check the following:

Is the text too technical for potential readers?
Is the tone appropriate for the task and topic (work, school, community)?
Is the text as short as it can be?
Are there varied sentence types?

To write clearly and effectively means that you must consider your audience, the readers. Are you writing for peers (colleagues, classmates), for experts, or for the general public? No matter whom you write for, a text that is easy to understand encourages more readers to find out about your ideas.

This section deals with style. How can you make your writing clear and easy for the reader to follow? Use the suggestions below only after you have written your first draft.

CONSIDER THE AUDIENCE

Make sure your text is appropriate for your **audience**—the kind of readers who will be reading your text. They may be classmates, teachers, experts in your field, or the general public. If you lose many readers because they have no idea what you are writing about, you have failed to communicate your ideas.

Your audience can vary and sometimes you may be writing for several types of readers. The following are possible groups of readers:

- Young adults

- Adults / general public

- Children under 10

- A person you are writing a formal letter to (for example, a director of personnel)

- Experts (scientists, accountants, psychologists)

- People with a specific interest (perhaps in photography, computers, planes)

Do not use technical or specialized terms with non-experts. For example, do not use physics equations to explain how gamma rays travel if your audience is made up of people who do not have a background in science. Think about how the audience for the first sentence differs from that of the second sentence.

1 Photosynthesis can best be described as $6H_2O + 6CO_2 \rightarrow C_6H_{12}O_6 + 6O_2$.

2 Photosynthesis can best be described as green plants using sunlight energy to release the oxygen we need to stay alive.

When you apply for a job, do not use very specific terms that are understood mostly by experts in your field. The director of personnel might not be familiar with the vocabulary for every type of job.

For instance, use an abbreviation only if you are certain that the readers understand it (*IBM* is a familiar example). Otherwise, you will make your text longer by having to explain the meaning.

Right (only if your readers know *URL*): We wanted to know if they had a URL.

Better: We wanted to know if they had an Internet address.

Workshop

With a partner, find out which of the following abbreviations are commonly understood.

AWOL	B.C.	B.C.E.	CEO	C.P.A.	CPR	GMO	GMT	GNP	GP	GPS
GST	I.D.	M.H.R.	NASA	PIN	P.M.	PR	R & D	SSN	SUV	WHO

USE APPROPRIATE TONE

Tone refers to whether a text is meant to sound, for example, business-like, scholarly or humorous. You must develop a sense of audience to be able to choose the tone that is appropriate for your type of readers.

Always adopt a polite tone. You never know who will someday be in a position to help you. Avoid an aggressive or unpleasant tone. Can you see the effect the following sentence may have on the reader?

⊗ I compared two projects that are ready for development and I think the second one is ridiculous.

Register means the type of language used in a particular situation or a specific type of writing. When confronted with a series of words with similar meanings, you must choose the appropriate word for a specific situation. For instance, if you work part-time in a store, some of the words you choose will differ from those you would use with your friends at a café.

In academic and work-related writing, certain terms occur either less or more often than they do in speaking. For example, terms such as *requesting* and *supply* are more commonly found in business writing than in everyday conversation.

Words that are acceptable in one context might not be correct in others:

⊗ To me, a mother is a girl who educates children.

To see how some terms are more appropriate in certain contexts, place the terms in the appropriate sentences. Discuss whether there are differences in meaning.

1 *get rid of / dispose of*

We'll have to figure out a way to _____ our dump of toxic chemicals.

Our company will respect environmental norms to _____ toxic chemicals.

2 *delay / hold up*

Sorry I am late. I was _____ in traffic.

Because of the storm, many flights were _____.

3 *remain silent / shut up*

You have the right to _____.

Why don't you just _____ for a change.

4 *kids / offspring*

How do parents pass their genes on to their _____?

She babysits a couple of _____.

CONNOTATION

The tone of a text can also be influenced by what a word suggests: its **connotation**. In addition to its basic meaning—called the **denotation**—a word can suggest an additional meaning through its connotation. Words with similar denotations, such as *caution* and *danger* (which can mean "be careful") take on different connotations with different levels of risk.

Fill in the missing words in the signs below to see the difference between *caution* and *danger*.

Workshop

With the help of a dictionary, discuss the differences in the pairs of sentences below.

1.1 How often has she **complained** before?

1.2 Is she always **whining** like that?

Who is richer?

2.1 My neighbor is **well-to-do**.

2.2 My brother-in-law is **wealthy**.

Who impressed the hiring committee?

3.1 **Sweat** rolled down her face throughout the interview.

3.2 Of course, it may happen that young women **glisten with perspiration** under stress.

4.1 **Make a list** of the problems.

4.2 **Maintain a record** of the problems.

5.1 He thought it was **brilliant**.

5.2 We thought it was **clever**.

6.1 My roommate watched a **whodunit** on T.V. last night.

6.2 For the final assignment, you are required to read three types of **mystery novels**.

E-MAIL TONE VS. LETTER STYLE

An e-mail message is usually more informal than a business letter, but you should still watch what you say.

- **Do not use language that is inappropriate in writing.**

   Don't write anything you might regret or that might land you up in court (hate mail, descriptions of sexual acts).

   ⊗ Hey Bob, I been too busy to write of late but I gotta tell you about the hot date I got last night.

   Four-letter words might be accepted in barroom conversations, but you probably would not want anyone to read a transcript of your private conversations.

- **Do not make negative comments about anyone.**

   ⊗ I can't stand my boss.

   Your boss may have access to your e-mail. Also, anything you write can be forwarded in a click to someone else.

BE AS SHORT AS POSSIBLE (AND AS LONG AS NECESSARY)

Why? Your job is to explain, not to show how many words you know. Studies show that the speed of reading from a computer screen is 25 percent slower than reading from paper. Write less, especially if your text is going to be read on screen.

How? Ask yourself the following four questions:

CAN YOU DELETE EMPTY WORDS?

⊗ In job interviews, ~~I guess that~~ it is important to look confident.

⊗ ~~I think that~~ more research is needed.

⊗ ~~As everybody knows,~~ almost one third of the pupils do not eat breakfast. (Why should you cut the beginning of this sentence? Either everybody knows what you are saying, so you don't have to remind them—or they don't know and will feel inadequate.)

Some words are empty because they repeat other words.

⊗ Of all the possibilities I have examined, I kept two ~~of them.~~ (*of them* = of all the possibilities; this part is obvious to the reader)

Practice

Cut any unnecessary words by crossing them out.

1 Me, personally, I think that we do not need to convince anyone.

2 The reason why I am writing is because we need additional information on the risk of water contamination.

3 There are many reasons that can explain a loss of power.

4 He had an idea that is a solution to our problem.

5 I think family and health matter more than money.

6 My opinion about that, and I mean about the definition of "mother" is clear.

7 I definitely believe that it is important to measure the effect of gases.

8 As everybody knows, it is a fact that cows produce methane.

CAN YOU REPLACE EMPTY WORDS SUCH AS *THERE IS/THERE ARE/IT IS?*

Using gerunds (*-ing*) can often help cut down the number of words.

    Long: In job interviews, it is important to look confident.

    Better: In job interviews, looking confident is important.

Now, try this one:

    It is necessary to hold a driver's license for this job.

Check if you can replace the verb *to be.* In some cases, when *to be* means "equal," it is hard to replace.

Our president is Ms. Norwalk. (Ms. Norwalk = president)

BUT: When *to be* introduces a place or an event, use a verb that makes the idea clear right away. This might cut down the length of the sentences that follow.

Paul was at the conference.

Better: *Paul spoke at? organized? attended?* the conference.

These are the steps that you must follow.

Follow these steps.

Practice

Rewrite the sentences without using *to be.*

1 Here is the new technique. It involves replacing missing teeth with a dental implant.

_____

2 This is a solution I prefer because it is easy for people to learn it. _____

_____

3 These are the tips you should follow when travelling in bear country. _____

_____

4 There were thirteen people who attended the meeting. _____

_____

CAN YOU USE THE ACTIVE VOICE OF THE VERB?

To be, this time as an auxiliary, or helping, verb, can disappear if you choose the active voice (the subject is the actor) over the passive voice (the subject does nothing + *to be* + past participle).

Long: As is presented in the graph, it can be noted that ...

Better: The graph shows ...

Practice

Can you shorten the following by changing the verbs from passive to active?

1 During the experiment, the temperature *was raised* to 50° and the changes *were noted*.

2 The survey *was administered* by telephone to a randomly selected sample of Canadian drivers. Opinion Search Inc. conducted the interviews in late March and early April, 2001.[1]

3 A quest *was launched* by Gandalf to destroy the ring.

CAN A NOUN-MODIFYING-NOUN CONSTRUCTION BE USED?

If possible, try to use a **noun-modifying-noun** construction (e.g., *computer screen*) or a **compound adjective** (e.g., *task-oriented*) instead of a long construction with prepositions. Non-modifying-noun constructions will help you write short subject lines in business letters or e-mails and create useful headings between the parts of your text. Compound adjectives are also common in technical and professional writing.

Examples:

1 The report, which has twenty-three pages, explains the plan in detail.

The *twenty-three-page* report explains the plan in detail.

2 The project, which is two years old , ...

The *two-year-old* project ...

Compound adjectives can be built with many types of combinations:

- a *risk-free* investment (noun + adjective)
- an *insurance-dictated* decision (noun + past participle)
- *crash-test* dummy (noun + noun)
- *long-held* belief (adverb + past participle)
- *intensive care* unit (adjective + noun)
- *low-flying* planes (adverb + present participle)
- The *play-by-play* broadcast of the game (noun + preposition + noun)

> **Usage Hint:**
> Compound adjectives often are formed with hyphens (-). In very common terms, the expressions often lose their hyphens:
> *social security system*
> *intensive care unit*

---

1. *The Road Safety Monitor: Driver.* http://www.trafficinjuryresearch.com/whatNew/newsItemPDFs/RSM_Driver_Distraction.

Part A. In scientific and technical writing, the writer will often place the main noun at the end of the combination. Change the following into three-word combinations that end with the noun that is in italics.

Example: a *robot* that is controlled from a remote spot: a _____ *remote-controlled robot* _____

1 a *strategy* to control the population: a _____

2 a *system* to ensure the security of our home: a _____

3 the *requirements* in terms of experience for a job: _____

4 a *program* that is friendly to the users: _____

5 the *regulations* of the department that protects us against fire: _____

6 *diseases* that are related to stress: _____

7 the *plant* where the filtration of water takes place: _____

8 the *procedures* needed for surgery on the heart: _____

Part B. Change the words in italics to their *-ing* form to build structures that end with the main noun in the following examples.

Example: a program that *processes* words (three words): _____ *word-processing program* _____

1 a session where people are *trained* (two words): _____

2 techniques used in *interviews* (two words): _____

3 water that we can *drink* (two words): _____

4 a factor that *unifies* (two words): _____

5 the company that *leads* the market (three words): _____

6 some research that *consumed* a lot of time (three words): _____

7 the process we use to *brew* beer (three words): _____

8 the committee that will *make* the decision (three words): _____

USE VARIED SENTENCE TYPES

Many readers find texts more effective when **simple**, **compound** and **complex** sentences bring variety to the writing.

If you use only simple sentences (containing just one subject and one verb), your readers might perceive your writing as immature.

⊗ I will talk about the importance of planting trees in cities. People find tree-lined streets attractive. Trees improve the air. They also create shade. Planting trees makes neighborhoods safer. More trees should be planted in urban areas.

Simple sentences are useful when you present a series of facts or statistics. They help make the information clearer. Each sentence below has one subject and one verb.

> How many crashes are attributable to fatigue? Estimates vary widely, from 3 percent in the United States, according to an American Medical Association study in 1998, to 25 percent in Australia, according to a 1991 study in the *Australian and New Zealand Journal of Medicine*.
>
> Canadian numbers are at the low end of the scale. Of the 401,572 collisions listed in the *Ontario Road Safety Annual Report* for 1999, only 1,744 were specifically attributed to fatigue. Alcohol and drug impairments accounted for another 4,700 and inattentiveness for 21,597. The rest were other, or unknown, causes.[2]

Compound sentences are composed of two independent clauses: each clause contains a subject and a verb. The clauses are joined by *and, or, but, then,* or *yet.* Compound sentences can help you show that the two ideas joined by the connector are equally important. Compound sentences are common in news reports.

> The dollar has dropped about 20 percent in the past two years, **and** at the current levels, it is somewhat undervalued. Over the same period, interest rates have been relatively steady, **but** we can expect an increase soon. Fortunately, our exports are on the upswing, **but** they cannot make up for the difference in the dollar exchange rate.

Practice

Turn the following into compound sentences by using *and, but,* or *or.*

1 To turn a profit, Air Naratoren has saved money by creating cheaper subdivisions. It bought new planes with lower fuel consumption.

2 A company must care about the environment. It must still make a profit at the end of the year.

3 To avoid shipping delays, you must order before the first of the month. You must also include a credit card number.

4 To increase production, our company could force employees to work the evening shift. We could switch to new technologies in the production process.

5 The story presents a depressing view of sexual roles. It tries to impose a traditional male-dominated view of the family.

Complex sentences are common in texts where analyses involve abstract ideas. For example, professional reports and academic essays often need to develop along a time sequence, to look at cause and effect, or to compare and contrast ideas. This often requires complex sentences.

A complex sentence is made up of one **main clause** that should contain the main point and at least one **subordinate clause**. The subordinate clause should show a less important idea whose meaning depends on the meaning of the main clause (subordinate clauses are also called **dependent** clauses).

MORE HELP? See Length of Sentences, p. 133 and Transitions, p. 85.

---

2. Winston, Iris. (2002, Feb. 22) "When the Best Remedy is Rest," *Ottawa Citizen.*

TYPES OF SUBORDINATE CLAUSES

This chart presents the major types of subordinate clauses and the connectors that show the type of relationship between a main clause and dependent clauses.

MAIN (OR INDEPENDENT) CLAUSES	TYPES OF SUBORDINATE (OR DEPENDENT) CLAUSES They do not give a complete idea if used alone.	CONNECTORS Here are connectors used to introduce each type of subordinate clause.
I really enjoyed the car →	**ADJECTIVE (OR RELATIVE) CLAUSES** Adjective clauses do the job of an adjective in that they add information to a noun (adjective clauses are also called **relative clauses**). *that the bank took back.*	*who, that, which, whose*
He stopped → dating his girlfriend Some people speak on their cell phones → Your order will → be late	**ADVERB CLAUSES** Adverb clauses can give information about time, place, condition, contrast, and cause and effect. *when he found out about the other man.* *wherever they are.* *since we had to close during the storm.*	• Time: *after; as; as soon as; before; once; since; when; whenever; while* • Place: *where; wherever* • Condition: *if; provided that; unless; whether* • Contrast: *although; even though* • Cause and effect: *as; because; since; so that*
It is unclear → I know → I'll go →	**NOUN CLAUSES** Noun clauses do the job of a noun. They can be a subject, object or complement. *why he asked for the car.* *that 25 percent of the students will fail.* *wherever you send me.*	• Fact: *that* • Place: *where; wherever* • Time: *when; whenever* • Reason: *why* • Condition: *if; whether* • Manner: *how; however* • Scope (number, frequency, duration …): *how much; how many; how often; how long; how soon; how late* • Choice: *whichever*

Practice

Combine the simple sentences below with connectors from the right-hand column in the chart on p. 144. This practice will help you to create complex sentences.

Example:

Create an adjective (or relative) clause:

We received a project for a new festival in Rockport. The project is too expensive.

The project that we received about a new festival in Rockport is too expensive.

Create an adjective clause:

1 The soil samples were taken at the gas station site. The site has been closed for over two months.

_____

_____

2 The bridge can carry more traffic than the old bridge. The bridge was built last year.

_____

Choose *although, if,* or *when* to create adverb clauses:

3 He was examining the possibilities. The machine broke down again.

_____

4 She was not in San Francisco at the time. The police thought she was a suspect.

_____

5 The president did not have access to privileged information. He would sell his shares in the company.

_____

_____

Choose *that, whichever, whatever* to create meaningful noun clauses:

6 _____ you say will be held against you.

7 _____ car I drive does not matter to me.

8 She confirmed _____ the meeting was postponed.

Workshop

In analyses, writers often use a variety of sentence types. Label each sentence *simple*, *compound* or *complex*.

Complex

[Although it is of course important that educational standards in schools should be carefully maintained, there is nothing to suggest that today's youngsters are less competent at speaking their native language than older generations of children were.] [Their ability to speak the language is just as good, and their ability to read and write is, almost certainly, a great deal better on average.] [Let's first consider the question of literacy.] [Is there any really persuasive evidence that literacy standards have declined?[3]]

[The setting of the novel in a poor district imposes limits to the characters' dreams.] [The depression has slowed down the construction business, and Azarius can no longer find work as a carpenter.] [In the working-class district, unemployed men like him walk from cafés to bars all day.] [His daughter, who works as a waitress, dreams of material possessions that, for many girls like her, can often be obtained only by marrying into the middle class.]

[Tai Chi is a martial art that promotes health and a sense of well-being.] [According to traditional Chinese medicine, the body contains a vital force called "chi."] [Tai Chi fosters the movement of chi throughout the body.] [There are different forms of Tai Chi, but all involve a series of gentle, graceful movements.] [Some forms consist of 105 movements, and other forms involve only 36.] [People who perform Tai Chi on a daily basis contend that doing the form increases their strength, circulation, flexibility, and balance.]

3. Milroy, James. (1998) "Children Can't Speak or Write Properly Any More" in *Language Myths*, Eds. Bauer, Laurie and Trudgill, Peter. Hammondsworth: Penguin, pp. 58-59.

APPENDIX
MODELS

Model Letter
Model Cover Letter
Model Job Résumé

200 Hempstead Turnpike
Garden City, NY 11530

January 4, 2005

Hercules A. Vance
Mickey's Mechanics
10 Verbena Avenue
Floral Park, NY 11001

Subject: TRANSMISSION

Dear Mr. Vance:

I bought a car from your used car lot on September 28th. It came with a 3-month warranty. Around Christmas time, I began hearing a rattle when I shifted into second gear. I went to have the car checked on December 27th. After an inspection, I was told by one of your mechanics that there was nothing wrong with the transmission and that it was just a little short on oil. There was no charge and no bill. Five days later, on January 1st, after the 3 month-warranty expired, so did the transmission. I had the car towed to your lot. When you opened on January 3rd, I was told that the transmission was shot. You asked me for $800 to fix it.

Because I had no written proof that I had come on December 27th, before the warranty expired, one of your employees refused to honor the warranty. As the problem was there before the warranty expired and your employees were unable to identify it, I want my car repaired at no cost. I have two witnesses who were with me in the car that day and will confirm the information. Please contact me to discuss the repairs.

Sincerely,

Melissa Repas

Melissa Repas

735 Maple Street
Moncton, New Brunswick
F4J 4M8
Canada

January 19, 2007

M.-E. Beaulieu
Human Resources Department
Big Sur University Hospital
2222 Big Sur Highway
Silicon, CA 90033
USA

Subject: ICU Nurse Position

Dear Ms. Beaulieu:

It was with great interest that I read your advertisement in the January
15th edition of *The Halifax Daily News*, describing employment opportunities in
nursing in the Intensive Care Unit of your hospital. I feel that my educational
background and professional experience meet the exact requirements for such
a job.

As you will see in the enclosed résumé, I have been working for the past
two years at the Moncton Hospital as a registered nurse trained for emergency
room situations. Prior to that, I developed speed, critical thinking, and clinical
skills while working at the Notre-Dame-de-la-Mer / Sea Hospital. The year that I
spent studying English at Cambridge was also an invaluable learning
experience. I successfully passed the "Cambridge Advanced English Exam" and
since then, I have become as proficient in English as in my native Vietnamese
and as in French, the language I went to school in.

I would very much like to work at Big Sur University Hospital because it is one
of California's most prestigious research and teaching facilities. Furthermore, I
have always loved the area, and I have been considering moving for the past few
years. I would be honored to be a member of your staff.

I would be pleased to provide you with any additional information in an
interview. Please feel free to contact me at this number: (506) 888-3727.

Sincerely yours,

Daphné Dinh

Daphné Dinh
Enclosurc: résumé

Nancy J. Grigg
100 Emmet Street
Charlottesville, VA 22904
Telephone: (434) 555-1143
njgrigg@dotnet.net

Position applied for: Camp Counselor

Education:

To be completed in May 2006
Bachelor's Degree in Psychology
University of Virginia, Charlottesville

June 2002
High School Diploma
Oscar F. Smith High School, Chesapeake

Experience:

September 2003-to date
Peer Tutor (English)
Assessed individual needs of first-year students, developed
corrective activities, provided instruction.
University of Virginia, Charlottesville

May 2003-August 2003
Day Camp Counselor
Supervised 12 children, coordinated bus pick-ups,
arranged outings.
Albemarle YMCA

June 2002-August 2002
Tourist Guide
Compiled and published historical information,
conducted tours, handled complaints, trained volunteers.
Monticello, The Home of Thomas Jefferson, Charlottesville

Skills:

Speak and write French, intermediate level
Speak Ukrainian, intermediate level
Can use most software such as Word, Excel, PowerPoint,
CorelDRAW, Photoshop, and Dreamweaver
Can design websites
Earned Level 1 as a Canoeing Instructor
Can play piano and guitar
Can type 50 words per minute

Other relevant experience:

Member of Chesapeake Chamber Music Players, 2000-2002
Writer and editor, student newspaper, 2000-2002: wrote
articles, edited copy, designed layout, oversaw distribution.

Awards:

Recipient of V. Thomas Forehand, Jr., Scholarship 2003-2004
Honor Roll, 2001 and 2002

References available upon request

INDEX